THE CREED BY

Tony Kelly has turned his depth of scholarship and clarity of expression to the central statement of traditional Christian belief: the Nicene Creed. Tony marries the attempt of early Christianity to state the TRUTHS of the Christian Faith with the way in which contemporary believers must make their own TRUTH of that statement. The Creed is to be learnt "by Heart". This does not mean rote memory, but a personal, communitarian, and intimate appropriation of all that God has done for the human condition in and through Jesus Christ.

This lucid book takes its reader through a reflection upon an age old expression of faith which enables that appropriation. In the end it is not what one knows that matters, but the way in which faith, enlightened and strengthened by reason, turns again to praise the God of Jesus Christ.

Francis J. Moloney, SDB, AM, FAHA
Professor of Theology
Australian Catholic University

M Mansum

Dec. 1997

Tony Kelly's most recent publications are *A New Imagining: Towards an Australian Spirituality* (Collins Dove), *Touching on the Infinite: An Exploration in Human Hope* (Collins Dove), *An Expanding Theology: Faith in a World of Connections* (E. J. Dwyer), and *Consuming Passions: Christianity and the Consumer Society* (Australian Catholic Social Justice Council).

THE CREED BY HEART

Re-learning the Nicene Creed

TONY KELLY, CSsR

HarperCollins*Religious*

HarperCollins*Publishers* AustraliaPty.Ltd.

Published by HarperCollins *Religious*
HarperCollins *Publishers* (Australia) Pty Ltd Group
17–19 Terracotta Drive
Blackburn, Victoria 3130, Australia
ACN 008 431 730

First published 1996
Text design by William Hung
Cover design by William Hung and Robert Klinkhamer
Typeset in 11/13pt Sabon by Kimberly Williams, Blue Orange
Printed in Australia by Griffin Press Pty. Ltd.

National Library of Australia Cataloguing-in-Publication data:

Kelly, Anthony, 1938– .
    The creed by heart: re-learning the Nicene Creed.

    ISBN 1 86371 596 7.

    1. Nicene Creed. I. Title.

238.142

CONTENTS

CONTENTS

FOREWORD

At the plenary meeting of the Australian Catholic Bishops' Conference following my ordination as a bishop in 1979, I was elected to the Bishops' Committee on Ecumenism. This happy event has led me over 17 years to a rewarding involvement in ecumenical affairs, in the Catholic Church and in other Churches and Christian Communities. It was against such a background that I took up Tony Kelly's work *The Creed by Heart*.

The Nicene Creed (so called) has been the subject of considerable interest in recent years. In 1981 Pope John Paul II wrote a letter to mark the 1600th anniversary of the First Council of Constantinople (381), which is generally thought to have given us the Nicene Creed as we now know it. He describes the Creed as 'the expression of the one common faith of the Church of the whole of Christianity' (Letter to the Bishops of the Catholic Church for the 1600th Anniversary, n.1). In 1992 the Catholic Church published *The Catechism of the Catholic Church*. The Nicene Creed provides the framework for the exposition of the faith of the Catholic Church in the first part of the Catechism.

In an explicitly ecumenical context, the most significant of these examples of renewed interest in the old Creed is the project of the Faith and Order Commission of the World Council of Churches, entitled Towards the Common Expression of the Apostolic Faith. This brave project, which was inaugurated in 1982, resolved to take the Nicene Creed as its points of reference. In 1991 the Commission was able to publish a collection of papers on its work entitled *Confessing the One Faith, An Ecumenical Explication of the Apostolic Faith as it is Confessed in the Nicene –Constantinopolitan Creed* (Faith and Order Paper No 153, Geneva 1991). This was in the nature of an interim report. The project is continuing.

We may ask: How important is this endeavour to arrive at a common confession of faith? To hold the faith of Jesus Christ in one's heart with love beyond measure and faithfulness that never fades is more important than any formula of words. And some followers of Jesus Christ are content to leave it at that. In their view creeds divide. However, from the start, long before Nicaea and Constantinople, the disciples of Jesus sought to have some tangible confession of words against which the genuineness of faith could be measured, for example on the occasion of a baptism. There are snatches of such confessions in the New Testament itself, and St Paul speaks of 'confessing with your lips as well as of believing in your heart' (Rom 10:9). Most churches and Christian communities have needed a creed, and still regard agreement in a commonly confessed faith as essential to unity.

But why the Nicene Creed? It is of course the best known and the most widely used of all creeds, even liturgically, in churches of both East and West. On the other hand, it is a document of its time. It makes no reference to certain matters which the churches would regard as integral to their faith, such as justification by faith, the Eucharist and episcopate. This is not to mention contemporary questions that have become urgent for all the churches but were not thought of, or mentioned, in the great fourth-century creed: the authority of the Church, proper esteem for the environment, gender equality, human generation, etc.

This very fact of the yawning gaps in the Nicene Creed from a contemporary standpoint helps us see its genuine role as an instrument of unity. It is not a case of counting the headings, as if a particular church or community may score so many out of ten. That was never the purpose of the Creed. It was rather a succinct summary of the whole faith. It was all that needed to be said. It was perfect. Any subsequent issue could be resolved by starting from the Creed. For unity of faith between the churches today nothing more is required than agreement on the Creed. The studies of faith and order are aimed at ensuring that we do indeed confess and understand it in the same way.

In this exercise it is extremely helpful if modern theologians will reflect on the Creed from a contemporary standpoint. This means starting from the issues that trouble modern people, believers and unbelievers alike, whether in mind or heart. To reflect on the Creed from that perspective is to see it as it was intended to be used. It enables us to get behind the words that were said into understanding why they were said, and what great Christian convictions were being protected in saying them.

This is the path followed in this work of Tony Kelly. I found it refreshing to look at the Creed through eyes of a modern and thoughtful believer, prepared to look at the 'Creator of Heaven and Earth' in the environment of modern science, and 'He Rose Again' in the light of historical–critical method. Reflection on the faith is never simple, but this exposition of the Creed is nonetheless straightforward and uncluttered by meticulous detail. Students of theology will find it a valuable introduction, and more experienced theologians will be given pause by the engaging remarks that characterize Tony Kelly's work. The unbeliever who wants to know in brief what Christians believe today will find it an invaluable summary.

It is a pleasure to commend it to readers. I wish them a journey satisfying by the enlightenment and the pleasure it brings.

BISHOP BEDE HEATHER
BISHOP OF PARRAMATTA

THE NICENE-CONSTANTINOPOLITAN CREED (381)

We believe in one God,
    the Father, the Almighty,
    maker of heaven and earth,
    of all that is, seen and unseen.

We believe in one Lord, Jesus Christ,
    the only Son of God,
    eternally begotten of the Father,
    God from God, Light from Light,
    true God from true God,
    begotten, not made,
    of one Being with the Father.
    Through him all things were made.
    For us [all] men and our salvation
        he came down from heaven:
    by the power of the Holy Spirit,
        he became incarnate from the Virgin Mary,
        and was made man.
    For our sake he was crucified under Pontius Pilate;
        he suffered death and was buried.
        On the third day he rose again
            in accordance with the Scriptures;
        he ascended into heaven
            and is seated at the right hand of the Father.
    He will come again in glory to judge the living and the dead,
        and his kingdom will have no end.

We believe in the Holy Spirit, the Lord, the giver of life,
    who proceeds from the Father (and the Son).
    With the Father and the Son he is worshiped and glorified.
    He has spoken through the Prophets.
    We believe in one holy catholic and apostolic Church.
    We acknowledge one baptism for the forgiveness of sins.
    We look for the resurrection of the dead,
        and the life of the [age] world to come. Amen.

1

INTRODUCING THE CREED

———

The Nicene-Constantinopolitan Creed, to give it its full name, is a classic statement of Christian faith. It has been so for over sixteen hundred years—its sixteenth centenary was celebrated in 1981. In its original Latin and Greek forms, despite the *filioque* controversies, this creed has had a long history as a symbol of unity between the churches of the East and West. Today, translated into many languages, this *symbolum fidei, symbolon pisteos*, is again being vigorously discussed as the basis for a new era of ecumenism.

Aware of the continuing ecumenical potential of the Nicene Creed, the World Council of Churches has completed a ten-year study of this ancient confession of faith.* The task is clearly not exhausted. There are so many new elements in the present-day discussion of the meaning of the creed. Obvious examples are the emerging role of women in both Church and society, the Church's public commitment to justice in the world, our common responsibility for the environment, protest against the increasing materialism of our day, inter-faith dialogue, and a fresh sense of the wonder of creation made possible by modern science. These are just a few of the new elements demanding a wider catholicity in any interpretation of the creed.

---

* *Confessing the One Faith: An Ecumenical Explication of the Apostolic Faith as it is Confessed in the Nicene-Constantinopolitan Creed (381)*, Faith and Order Paper No. 153, WCC Publications, Geneva, 1991.

APPROACHING THE CREED

My concern here is not to re-issue what dozens of excellent theological studies and hundreds of ecumenical meetings have recorded. While I am obviously influenced by such explorations, this meditation on the creed has a quite simple aim. By focusing on the basic meaning of the creed we will have a chance to learn it again "by heart," so to speak. The challenge is to present the creed as a felt whole, the way a favorite poem or song is learned and becomes a permanent and deep possession. I am presuming that the Christian community will quite properly continue to experiment with fresher and more telling ways of expressing the central tenets of its faith. Still, the Nicene Creed has a classic status, for it serves as both an inspiration and a norm for any further experiment. Any effort on the part of faith to re-think or re-learn its classic expressions cannot but widen the possibilities of Christian expression. Certainly such efforts, despite our different needs, traditions, styles and languages, can only enrich our communication in what most unites us in mind and heart and life.

I have deliberately chosen a more openly reflective style of expression, perhaps closer to prayer than the technical expressions of theology. By getting a feel for the creed as a whole and in its various parts, we can come to a keener appreciation of how it is a *formula*—literally, a "little form"—of the limitless reality of the love that has found us and called us together.

THE CREED WITHIN HISTORY

The creed is a product of its time, in the centuries that went into its making. Different cultures, languages, conflicts, and historical situations have left their mark. Very early in the history of Christian faith it was realized that a mere repetition of biblical formulae was not enough. There was always the question of differing interpretations. And so, if the Church were to keep what it considered—or came to consider—as the real meaning of the scriptural witness to Christ, it soon found that it had to be involved in an ongoing work of re-interpretation. If it was to hold true to the original faith in all its simplicity and life-giving power, the Church had to experiment in expressing itself in languages and modes of cultural expression quite different from the speech and times of the New Testament period.

The Nicene Creed is a significant instance of such a historical experiment; and the fact that it continues to be used these sixteen centuries later makes it a highly successful one. Within the genre of creeds, it is a comparatively complex and highly developed statement of Christian belief. Born of a history of conflict, it represents a considerable learning experience. Because this creed represents an effort "to get it all together," it comes down to us as something like a resolution passed at the end of a long and difficult meeting.

There were, of course, other and simpler creeds, usually employed in a baptismal setting. The best known one is the Apostles' Creed. But all creeds arose out of the need to give simple expression to what believers believe in. When the focus is clear, the communication is more sure. Clarity and brevity are of the essence in communicating anything of importance. It is not helpful to refer the newly baptized to a theological treatise and those gathered for the eucharist did not come for a philosophical symposium.

This creed, and others like it, had their origins in a natural drive to precision and brevity. As instanced in many passages of the New Testament, standard "short formulae" were already in existence from the earliest times. For example, Paul could say "I handed on to you as of first importance what I in turn had received: that Christ died for our sins in accordance with the scriptures, and that he was buried, and that he was raised on the third day ... " (1 Cor 15:3 f.); and much later:

He was revealed in the flesh
vindicated by the Spirit
seen by angels,
proclaimed among Gentiles,
believed in throughout the world,
taken up in glory. (1 Tim 3:16)

Presumably such expressions were sung or recited in liturgical or catechetical settings well before the actual composition of the New Testament writings themselves (cf. 1 Cor 8:6, 12:3; Mk 8:29; Mt 28:19; Rom 1:3–5, 8:34; 1 Pet 3:18–20; 1 Tim 3:16). The effort to crystalize the expression of faith was a necessary part of witnessing to the decisive occurrence of what had happened in Christ. A blessed brevity and vividness had its place in the proclamation of "The Good News."

But there was also need, in the course of history, for a blessed explanation and articulation of the key points. Once the Gospel began to be explored in accordance with the great philosophical tradition, new questions began to be formulated. Of course, neither Jesus himself nor the New Testament writers were intent on giving theology seminars. Their aim was conversion. They sought to instill a new sense of life in the face of death, guilt, fear, and cosmic darkness. In that sense they appealed directly to the heart. But there would be a time for mind, a time for intelligence to catch up with what was disclosed to the heart. And that time came comparatively quickly as Christianity took root in the Greco-Roman world. The long history of what we call theology begins. Now faith is subjected to intellectual scrutiny and theoretic ordering. At one time, an expression of the Trinity as three "modes" or "appearances" of the one God might pass as a serviceable, rather rough and ready way of speaking about the Three. But later, when such imagery is pressed into intelligence, former simple explanations risk trivializing the unique event of God's self-communication in Christ. Similarly, a living sense of faith, as yet untroubled by theoretical concerns, could live with both the Johannine statements "The Father and I are one" (Jn 10:30) and "the Father is greater than I" (Jn 14:28). But there would come a time when the precise question could be posed: Is the one who is Jesus truly located in the divine realm, or is he one part, however noble, of creation itself?

A philosophical acumen develops within the tradition of believing. Believers begin to ask, Just what does this mean? How am I to believe it? The process of reflection was made more urgent by the taunts of sophisticated pagan contemporaries. These were not slow to point out that all this business about God having a son, and being born of a virgin, dying and rising, and so forth, was just a re-issue of the well-known mythologies that any serious philosophy had long left behind. Similarly, to keep its continuity with the tradition of Jewish faith while preserving the culminating character of the Christ as fulfillment of the ages, the question of the one God had to be faced in a new way. How could Jesus be truly divine if both Jew and Christian were dealing with the one God who called Abraham, inspired the prophets, and promised the Messiah and the salvation of the nations?

And so Christian thinkers had to face new inevitable questions if their faith was to make sense in the real world of their best thinking and urgent confrontations. Gradually questions could be chiseled into very precise forms to which Yes/No answers were required: Is Jesus truly God, or is he created? Is he is truly divine? If so, is he truly human? Is the God of the Church the same as the God of Israel? These and similar questions brought home to the Christian believers of the first centuries that their faith had to be continually interpreted if its radical simplicity was to remain intact. Indeed, further fundamental questions were implied: How were the scriptures to be interpreted? And, who, finally was to do the interpreting?

The fact of such questions being asked and answered affects the wording of the Nicene Creed, as we shall see. In an atmosphere of fierce debate and confused terminology, councils were called to thrash out the truth of the matter and to identify errors and distortions. Eventually, those with a care for the unity of the Church had to propose, in each case, a viable reconciling formula as a pattern for future instruction and theological exploration.

Hence, the Nicene Creed represents a certain accumulation of learning experiences in the understanding of the faith. The integrity of Christian faith demanded that it state, against the Gnostics, that God was the maker of everything, not just of spiritual reality; and against Arius, that Jesus as the Son of God was not made, but begotten, that he was "of one Being with the Father"; and, against those slow to accept the full trinitarian reality of God, that the Holy Spirit was truly divine and not just an impersonal creative or created force.

This creed took shape, then, in those first four hundred years of Christian reflection. It was drawn up to counter any regression to a more vague position, and to maintain the radical novelty of Christian revelation against those who would reduce it to something else in terms of a philosophical system or of the vivid imagery of popular mythology. For the creed planted the seeds of a distinctive intellectual conversion in which the mind would serve but not dominate the revealed mystery. Christian doctrine had now to crystalize realities of faith that had previously been kept in solution.

The Nicene Creed is of historic importance in two senses. First, it was the outcome of a particular history of conflict and confusion. Secondly, its achievement was of decisive importance in the ages to come. We can find in it a sense of continuing interaction with the past, for it accents the oneness of God and the role of the scriptures and the prophets of Israel. It gives evidence of facing the challenge to meet the demands of a new cultural situation, as it rejects any polytheistic and mythological connotations of paganism. At the same time, in its readiness to learn from a philosophical tradition of critical thinking, faith was enabled to employ technical terms and expressions to clarify its meaning.

To that degree, the creed is an instance of how faith is inculturated. While witnessing to the novelty of Christian reality to the culture of the Mediterranean world, Church doctrine had to use the best resources the culture had to offer in thinking out and defining what faith really meant. In so doing, it planted the seeds of new intellectual creativity that, in the course of time, would bring forth a Christian civilization.

THE NEED FOR A CREED
In a way, the need for a creed is a special characteristic of Christianity. At the heart of such a faith is the culminating event of the incarnation, in the life, death, and resurrection of Christ. If the Word of God had become flesh among us, then that momentous event meant something; and it must be kept in clear

focus. Hence, clear verbal formulae were needed to affirm the uniqueness of what had occurred. Indeed, because of its incarnational sense, Christian faith exhibits a certain confidence in words and definitions in ways that contrast with other faiths. The Church can word its faith because God has worded saving revelation in the Word made flesh.

Today, after the passage of so many centuries, believers are experiencing a considerable difficulty. Faith has become so qualified and even complicated in its expression. This is the main reason for the growing interest in re-examining this great creed, to find a source of unity. When our different traditions and theologies, having once grown apart, are now converging in a new ecumenism, a re-learning of the creed—"by heart," if you like—is a positive act of hope.

RE-LEARNING THE CREED

"Learning by heart" contrasts with both ritual recitation and theological speculation. When neither mind nor heart is involved, the various articles and phrases of the creed become increasingly disjointed. With no vital interlinking of the parts, there can be no integrated sense of the whole and there is a loss of sharp focus in the essential meaning of faith. Without such a recovery of its deep meaning, the creed becomes increasingly foreign, exotic and mystifying in its ancient words and formulations. Without a sense of the underlying coherence of the creed, we cannot be in a position to mean it anew in a fresh and engaging way. Though the mystery remains—God's saving love is ever undiminished—the world behind this creed is now vanished, and its original languages are no longer living. It comes to us out of a world far different from our own, just as it is translated into languages today that previous generations of Christians could never have known.

To earlier times, the creed's confident confession of "one God" as the ultimate source and goal of all was the least problematic of its statements. But in today's culture, such a statement is defiant: it flies in the face of the deeply atheistic and agnostic suppositions of the modern world. A huge shift in consciousness has occurred. Once pagan, Jew, Christian and

Gnostic all shared a religious world-view in which the reality of one God as the one ultimate truth could not conceivably be doubted. In such a time, conflict between various religious stances turned on how that one reality could be known, and on how it had revealed itself. Today, however, the reality of God has become the question—or, perhaps, not even a question—to a vast number of our contemporaries who, culturally speaking, are numbed as regards any religious sense of reality.

Imagine the change in this way. Say you lived in a house on the seashore, where the windows opened onto a large vista of sky, sea, and sweeping coast. The view is comparatively unimpeded: you can see the sun in the sky, where the sky meets the sea, where the waves break on the coast sweeping off into the distance. But then, either through erosion or earthquake, the solid earth shifts. The foundations of your house move; it begins to tilt uncomfortably downward toward a ravine filled with the wreckage of other collapsing buildings. The windows of your house are still there, even if the glass is shattered; but now there is no view of sky, ocean, and land, and how they meet. From the sloping floor of the room, if you look out the window you can see only the eroded earth. To get some sense of your former view, you would have to squat down and look upward through the upper pane of the cracked glass. The former open view is no longer a harmonious prospect, but a fleeting glimpse made possible only by a nimble balancing act—creeping to the window and looking upward from the sloping floor through the shattered panes. So too our cultural point of view has changed. With that, there is the urgent need to reconstruct, relocate, and salvage what building materials we can in an effort to rebuild the sturdy house of faith for future generations.

You could put it another way. We need to "deconstruct" the creed as an external set of traditional words if we are going to reconstruct it in the liveliness of personal faith. Words and phrases like "God," "maker," "Almighty," "heaven and earth," "seen and unseen," "Lord," "Light from Light," "salvation," "came down from heaven," "resurrection," "ascension," "come again," cannot simply be looked up in some kind of comprehensive dictionary, even though such an act of elementary research will certainly have its place. But if this "looking up" is all we do, we are stuck with an ancient meaning that someone else, the compiler of the dictionary, has decided for us. In contrast, a living faith has first to ask itself: What are we now trying to say in these words, and why? We are under the necessity of recovering the original sense of the great reality that gave rise to all the various articles of faith. Without a genuinely living sense of faith in the present, we cannot appreciate even the most venerable formulations of faith from the past. That might seem to imply that we have lost our grip on what before seemed so solid and precise. Faith seems to be left tongue-tied before the questions, What do you really mean? What do you really believe in? How is God present to you?

Nevertheless, such vertigo can be healthy. A temporary loss of bearings, a disconcerting disorientation, makes us appreciate all the more the solid substance of the creed. We begin to discover it afresh, as a way of "getting it all together" in a world of so many shifting parts—but now with a greater allowance for the play of many possible meanings in the presence of the mystery of grace that continues to draw us to itself. Believing now entails a deeper sense of personal responsibility. The creed today promises no free ride. Our beliefs have to be re-learned "by heart," if they are to resonate from within as expressions of ultimate meaning and promise. Most of all, the words of faith have to be backed by works of love and justice. If they are not world-transforming words, our faith is edged out of the world-in-the-making into increasing impotence: "Not everyone who says to me, 'Lord, Lord,' will enter the kingdom of heaven, but only the one who does the will of my Father in heaven" (Mt 7:21).

On the other hand, the restlessness of human intelligence with all its variety of viewpoints, to say nothing of the conflict of human feelings and concerns, predictably tries to fill what often is experienced as a vacuum of meaning. Believers can jump to conclusions and so arrive at judgments that are too simplistic, rigid, and exclusive of other points of view. This is the source of heresy, of *haeresis*, of being fixated in one aspect of faith at the expense of the whole saving sense of proportion. In contrast, the creed works to keep returning faith to the central issue of God and of the totality of the salvation offered us. It represents the delicate balance of "orthodoxy"—the right sense of proportion—in contrast to any lopsided bias, just as "catholic"—openness to the whole—is in contrast to rigid exclusivism. Admittedly, there is a risk here as well. For it is never a matter of idolizing a formula, but of always adoring and participating in the living reality the creed articulates.

The problem for all expressions of faith is to illumine and invite to the inexpressible, yet not to replace it. But by re-learning the creed "by heart" in the sense described we can prevent it from being turned into either an idolatrous projection of our own perceptions or an ideological instrument of our own securities. We are less likely to be "peddlers of God's word" (2 Cor 2:17) and more likely to be responsible stewards of God's mysteries (1 Cor 4:1). Learned "by heart," the creed becomes an icon, a sacred form in a holy space. Through it, the great mystery is allowed to reveal itself. The creed is like the open hand of faith holding the living lizard of the whole truth. In this way, we are not left merely with the creature's tail because of an over-eager attempt to catch it in some kind of intellectual system.*

THE LIMITS OF THE CREED

There is, of course, a basic objection: no one formula of faith is ever adequate; it leaves out so much. It is strange how what was unproblematic in those early centuries tended to be left out or taken for granted. But it is precisely that unproblematic, taken-for-granted atmosphere of faith that is most important. In the inexpressible wholeness of faith the words of the creed do their work in the service of a divine presence and so orientate our lives. The creed means far more than the sum total of its words or of the theological words that might seek to expand and explore its meaning. What the creed fully means can never be simply "looked up" in a theological dictionary.

* I owe this example, originally suggested in Turgenev's letter to Tolstoy, to Frans Jozef van Beeck, *God Encountered I : Understanding the Christian Faith,* Harper & Row, San Francisco, 1989, p. 17.

What are some of these "givens" in the world of faith that are not actually expressed, but powerfully affect the way we interpret a creed such as this? Most obviously, there is the reality of divine love that is revealed in Christ and summons us to participate in its life and scope: "Be merciful, just as your Father is merciful" (Lk 6:36). By quoting that saying of Jesus in the Gospels, we are reminded of another thread of the living texture of faith that is not included in the creed: there is nothing about the actual human life of Jesus, about what he did in his healings, exorcisms, miracles, and meals. Nor is there any explicit reference to what he said, either in prayer or parable, in commandment or prophecy. Further, there is no mention of the context in which we are most likely to recite this creed together, namely the eucharist, the sacrament of unity *par excellence*. Indeed, there is no reference in the creed's orthodoxy to the "orthopraxy" (right acting) of Christian life, presumably expressed in Godly generosity, forgiveness, peace-making, and living justly. Yet without such, Christian faith would be hardly recognizable.

Clearly, no creed, not even this venerable and most comprehensive ecumenical creed, can express the whole substance of Christian life. While the boundless mystery of saving love cannot be hidden—God continues to be revealed—it cannot simply be fully told or held in any formula. It is one thing to have a hope that opens the heart to anticipate a universal fulfillment. It is another matter to fill that expectation with definitions marked with the limitations of a provisional world. Even as all words fail, the mystery remains.

Here the scriptures themselves teach us the special virtues of reserve and patience in regard to the expression of faith. For all the explicitness of their promise of eternal life, for all the variety of images they employ, the biblical writers know what to leave unsaid. Faith cultivates its own tact. The biblical word of God is familiar with a double silence in the story of salvation: the silence of the Lord's death and the silence of his resurrection. One is a dark silence when the voice of Jesus is stilled. The other is a luminous silence when faith trembles in the presence of the new creation. Though the paschal mystery of the cross and resurrection of the Lord remains the basic parable of Christian existence, it takes none of the waiting or wonder out of our faith: "What no eye has seen, nor ear heard, nor the human heart conceived, ... God has prepared for those who love him" (1 Cor 2:9).

Surrounding the intimate awareness of faith there is, to borrow the title of a great mystical classic, "a cloud of unknowing." Compared to our human judgments, the ways of God are inscrutable just as divine judgments are unsearchable (Rom 11:33). Christian theology has to learn the discretion of a *theologia negativa*, the way of negation and waiting, if it is to serve as an authentic expression of faith. We may not settle for any provisional version of human identity, however advanced that might be, for "what we will be has not yet been revealed" (1 Jn 3:2). We cannot turn history into a human plan, since it is not given to us to know the conditions of the times and the seasons of God's initiative (Acts 1:7). Faith prepares us to meet the future, rather than to foretell it.

Even as hope becomes a passionate expectation of our resurrection in Christ, our understanding can only back into what is coming to be: what is "perishable, dishonorable, weak, physical" will become, through the creative power of the Spirit, "imperishable, glorious, powerful, spiritual" (cf. 1 Cor 15:42–44). Christian hope goes beyond its capacity to understand, to await a fulfillment in the one who "by the power at work within us is able to accomplish abundantly far more than all we can ask or imagine" (Eph 3:20). Our ultimate union with God must not be allowed to be reduced to any category within the present sphere of our experience: "hope that is seen is not hope" (Rom 8:24).

Thus, the scriptures provide a wholesome lesson. Hope expands to its proper proportions only within "the cloud of unknowing." In the darkness of faith, the Spirit is present in our hearts as the energy of expectation and desire: "for we do not know how to pray as we ought, but [the] Spirit intercedes for us with sighs too deep for words" (Rom 8:26). John's Gospel presents Jesus as saying that it is "to your advantage that I go away"— evidently to make room for a Spirit-guided history—"... for if I do not go away, the Advocate will not come to you; but if I go, I will send him to you" (Jn 16:7). As given to the disciples, this Spirit will declare "the things that are to come" (Jn 16:13).

Faith does well to remember this biblical conviction of darkness and waiting. Even our most treasured ways of speaking about God, as we are reminded by the Fourth Lateran Council (1215), must be aware of the gap between our images and the reality: "For between Creator and the creature no similitude can be expressed without implying a greater dissimilitude."*

Our profession of faith, then, operates within a field of meaning that can never be fully articulated. In all such expressions there is a tacit depth and sense of the divine without which religious words would echo in a vacuum. They presuppose a movement of life that, when all is said and done, can only be described as love—love received and love given—outside of which there is no true knowledge of God: "Beloved, let us love one another, because love is from God; everyone who loves is born of God and knows God ... for God is love" (1 Jn 4:7–8).

However valued the creed might be, it hardly pretends to be a compendium of the whole of Christian truth. If "the world itself could not contain the books that would be written" (Jn 21:25) to express the meaning of the Word made flesh, it would be unwise to expect the creed to express everything that Christ was, is, and will be for successive generations of Christians throughout the world, in all its history, and in all the variety of cultures. Compared to the whole Christian truth as it lived, prayed, and confessed, the creed is evidently a very limited and austere expression. Yet while it can look like the gnarled trunk of an old tree, we must still not forget how deeply its roots sink into holy ground and how precious is the fruit it bears.

---

*J. Neuner and J. Dupuis (eds.), *The Christian Faith: Doctrinal Documents of the Catholic Church*, 5th edition, HarperCollins*Religious*, London, 1992, p. 117.

2

THE MEANING OF THE CREED

Though this creed is a classic emblem of Christian orthodoxy, its meaning does not reside in mere recitation or incantation. The authentic rule of faith must have a deeper source. If it is not from the heart, with the full play of faith's experience and meaning, even the most sacred articulations of the faith can congeal into something odd and external, and actually block the character of faith as a radically personal act.

Still, the creed remains a verbal formula, arising out of deep experience and cultivation of the Christian mysteries. If experience gives rise to the words of the creed, those words point the way into inexhaustible depths of shared experience. As that experience is enriched in prayer and thought and action, new verbal expression is inspired. Conversely, as the experience of faith is worded, as it is made more telling, our capacities to enter into the all-demanding experiment of faith are enlivened. This is not unlike the expression of love; for the exchanges of love come out of, and lead into, new ways of loving.

A HOLISTIC READING

So, before looking at the three main articles of the creed and their various components, it is important to stress what we might call the holistic nature of this expression of faith. Quite simply, all its parts interpenetrate. The "one God" of its opening sentence is the Father of the Son and the Source of the Spirit. The Church is the assembly of those baptized in the name of the Father, Son, and

Spirit, just as the life of the world to come is the final state of being enfolded into the trinitarian communion. Both the resurrection of Jesus and the resurrection of the dead are the work of "the Father, the Almighty." And the "for us ... and our salvation" pervades every phrase and element. Just as the three divine persons are united in one community of life, so the three main articles of the creed, dealing with the Father, Son, and Spirit respectively, are coherent in one field of meaning. Faith does not speak of the Father without also implying that he is revealed in the Son and Spirit. Likewise, we cannot adore the Spirit save as the third divine person in relation to the other two. The totality is one of relationships: "The grace of the Lord Jesus Christ, the love of God, and the communion of the Holy Spirit" (2 Cor 13:13).

Though there is an ordered sequence of "articles" of faith, the creed is more like a hologram. Each article is related to the rest, and is explicable only in relation to the others. The "seen and unseen" totality of God's creation is the Christened universe: "Through him all things were made." To that degree, each article could be a starting point from which to elaborate the whole meaning of faith. The whole is contained in each, and each is part of the whole. Not to recognize that would result in the incoherent splintering of what was meant to be grasped as a whole.

While nothing worthwhile in human speech can be stated all at once, it can still be meant, however tacitly, as a living totality. Though the song has to be sung note by note, it is held together in a melodic unity and is supported by a sustaining breath. The one "Light from Light" diffracts into the various colors of its spectrum.

But the creed is a totality of a special kind. Its unifying factor, its fundamental field of meaning, can be nothing but the Christian confession, "God is love" (1 Jn 4:8), enacted in the self-giving of Christ, and enfolding all creation to itself. In this fundamental field of meaning there are seven key terms: Father, Son, Cross, Resurrection, Spirit, Church, and "the life of the world to come." Though such terms can be translated in different ways and be differently ordered, the creed opts for its own distinctive sequence in articulating the truth of love. A word, then, on each of them:

1   **Father.** In this name, God is love in a primordial and ultimate way, as the all-inclusive and all-encompassing source of all that is. An original love precedes all human effort and all created structures and dynamisms. Such love is the purely, sheerly, limitless "given" in relation to all Christian life and action—and indeed for "all that is ..."

2   **Son.** God is love in a unique self-utterance and self-expression. In the incarnation, a climactic self-involvement of God in creation takes place. Here God is not so much doing something for us and our salvation, but becomes a "someone" with us: God-with-us as the Word made flesh. God so loves the world as to give what is most intimate to the divine being and most expressive of the divine identity into the flesh of our existence: "This is my Son, the Beloved; listen to him!" (Mk 9:7).

3   **Cross.** God is love in an unconditional manner through the cross. At the point where the evil of human history is most manifest in crucifying the Son, there love keeps on being love as limitless mercy: "Father, forgive them; for they do not know what they are doing" (Lk 23:34).

4   **Resurrection.** God is love in a victorious manner through the resurrection of the Crucified One. The love of God is not defeated by the power of evil and death. It triumphs in raising Jesus from the dead, to glorify the Son as the true form and source of life for all.

5   **Spirit.** God is love as communicative in the Spirit. The love that has originated in the Father, and been incarnate in the life, death, and resurrection of the Son, is now breathed into history as a field of new life. It comprehends every time and place and people. In the Spirit, "the Lord and giver of life,"Christ is conceived, the Church brought into being, and all creation moves in a new energy to await its fulfillment.

6   **Church.** God is love as embodied in the historical reality of the "People of God." In the community of believers, baptized into the death and resurrection of Christ Jesus, nourished by his body and blood, and animated by his Spirit, the love of God is expressed. In the pilgrim, sacramental reality of the

Church, the saving mystery is celebrated and offered to the world. In its community and mission, the Church is an open circle, living and witnessing to the universal grace of love at work in all lives. To that degree, the Church is that part of the world and creation that is alive to the extent of God's love.

7 **"The life of the world to come."** God is love in bringing creation to its fulfillment. The love of God that had time for the emergence of the world and for the whole drama of human freedom will reach the final moment of its consummation "so that God may be all in all" (1 Cor 15:28). God is love, to use a theological term, "eschatologically."

Through these seven key terms, the creed elaborates the divine reality of self-giving love: "God sent his only Son into the world so that we might live through him" (1 Jn 4:9).

By accenting the mystery of the one God as the one self-giving and saving love, we are not only affirming the biblical foundation of the creed, but also precluding any temptation to use the creed in the repressive, divisive, or fundamentalist ways that often masquerade as orthodoxy. Authentic orthodoxy not only confesses the content of the creed centered in God's reconciling love, but also exhibits the style, so to speak, of such loving. Though the Nicene formula never once expressly mentions love by name, it is from beginning to end, in form and in substance, in origin and aim, entirely ordered to praise the glory of the "Father of our Lord Jesus Christ ... [who] chose us in Christ before the foundation of the world to be holy and blameless before him in love ... to the praise of his glorious grace that he freely bestowed on us in the Beloved" (Eph 1:3–6), to mark us with "the seal of the promised Holy Spirit, ... to the praise of his glory" (Eph 1:13–14). Right believing and right action are ultimately governed by the divinely original and final love articulated in the creed.

THE GRACE OF THE CREED

If the articles and elements of the creed are disconnected from the sweep of the total meaning of the creed, they are falsified. The creed itself arises out of and returns to the whole pulsing momentum of the life of the Church. Only by being immersed in the living experience of faith do the words of the creed mean anything. Apart from the praying, loving, hoping life of Christian faith, the creed is paper-thin.

However, the recognition of the living presence of God is not the outcome of some prior human skill or powers of perception on our part, somehow resulting in a fabrication of religious statements. Faith is knowledge of God born of the gift of grace: "In this is love, not that we loved God but that he loved us and sent his Son to be the atoning sacrifice for our sins" (1 Jn 4:10). Hence, believing is responding to the mystery that has disclosed itself: "No one can come to me unless drawn by the Father ..." (Jn 6:44). God's prior love, drawing us to Christ, is the great presupposition in all faith and in all expressions of belief. Without it, any creed would be meaningless incantation.

Just as a loved and familiar face is recognised in a crowd because of the million associations and feelings connected with it, so the words of the creed delineate, in a crowded world of words, only what is previously and deeply known.

The creed, then, works its meaning within an experience of "life to the full" (cf. Jn 10:10). That peculiar fullness is nothing other than participation in the "love-life" that God is. By dwelling in that source of life, by actively participating in its intimacy and overture, by celebrating and testing that vital reality in the community of the Church, the various expressions of the creed are given flesh and substance. Their meaning is never exhausted until the life of the world to come.

THE CREED AS PERSONAL CONFESSION

The creed starts with "We/I believe" and ends with "Amen." It is a personal statement made within a community of believers, backed by the Amen of their self-commitment. The credal formula occurs in the context of a shared set of beliefs expressed in word and deed, in hymns and in action, from generation to generation. To re-learn the creed by heart means bringing these words into contact with silences that words can never express, with the space that our human expression can never fill, with the unsayable depth out of which all statements of commitment emerge. In his letter to the Ephesians, Ignatius of Antioch writes, "It is better to be silent and real, than to talk and be unreal ... Whoever truly possesses the word of Jesus can also hear his silence"(chapter 15, vv. 1–2).

Obviously the creed articulates a judgment of belief *in* the mysteries. But that judgment is always made *out of* the convictions lying deep within the conscious, embodied, time-bound selves we are. In reality, believers in every age have to learn the creed by heart if they are to take their place in the great history of faith, and so "re-member" all the scattered elements of their lives and history in the light of the one common faith.

This is to say that the creed has to be appropriated, personally and communally, if its meaning is to be disclosed. Early forms of this and other creeds—still used at the Easter vigil and at baptism—put the creed in question form: "Do you believe ... ?" It demands a present, personal response: "Yes, we do believe." The declaration of the articles in an objective manner, "from the outside in," depends on a living assent to each of them "from the inside out." The creed expresses *the* faith only in relation to the personal act of *our/my* believing. Take the faith away and we are left to our inventions, projections, and opinions. Take *our/my* believing away and we are left with a detached, congealed formula. The two poles must come together in any living profession of Christian faith.

In this way, every expression of faith arises out of a knowledge born of participation in the revealed reality. By dwelling in that reality, by indwelling the wholeness of Christian truth, we bring it, part by part, to expression. To that degree, the creed is not a catalog of various items of information which the believer takes or leaves. Still, it is information in a deeper sense: the realities we assent to are known only as informing, and, indeed, as transforming, the communal and individual lives of believers. Like the eucharist, the creed has to be ingested, eaten and drunk, assimilated into our living existence, if it is to be truly held and confessed.

The cultural mentality of today is so fixated on an appreciation of knowledge as commodified information that we find it difficult to understand a deeper view of knowing in a much more personal sense. As a personal activity, all worthwhile knowledge arises out of deep self-investment in the search for truth. Truth emerges as the outcome of a commitment to a continuing learning through the whole scope of human experience.

A suggestive instance of such a participative mode of knowing is the blind person's white cane (both the physicist Niels Bohr and the philosopher of science Michael Polanyi have used this example). If I am visually handicapped, the stick is of immense benefit in tapping and feeling my way through the contours of the world around me. But I must hold it firmly enough to sense the shape of things, so that it is felt as an extension of my hand and arm. If I hold it too loosely, the long stick becomes an impediment, more likely to trip me up than to help me find my way around. At the other extreme, if I hold it too tightly, the cane will be merely a rigid extension of groping hand and body; it will not have sufficient "give" to feed back to my touch the turns and bends and drops and rises of the path ahead of me.

The courage and skill of the blind in their use of such a cane are a model for all our knowing. About the fullness of reality, we are all in the dark. But wherever we start on our path to the larger world of reality, we begin with the white stick of our prior beliefs, experience, hopes. It is the only way forward. Whether I am a scientist, an artist, or even a mystic, I am never a pure spectator: I am plunged already into what is, participating in it, indwelling it, moving within it. I always have "something to go on with"; and going on with this, firmly yet open to ongoing feedback, is the only way to go.

So, the creed. It is faith's white stick in dealing with the transcendent mysteries in which we are already immersed. It might be lengthened, or shortened, or differently weighted as the feedback continues; but it remains the way forward into a deeper knowledge of the realities that faith explores.

Extensions of this metaphor come to mind. The formula of marriage vows or religious consecration functions the same way. I cannot know or find the truth of what I have given myself to unless through a self-commitment. We can't stand outside and say, "I will see if it works." The deeper decisions of life demand the total involvement of "throwing ourselves into it." That is what participative knowing means: a constant, committed indwelling of the realities we hold as most true. The creed lives from such a way of knowing. Though we do not "see" the realities of faith all at once in this life, a confident, prayerful searching is the only way to become familiar with what God has revealed.

As a result, the creed is an expression of truth only for those who participate in the shared life of faith. By intimately collaborating in the community of faith, hope, and love, the meaning of God's indwelling in our hearts is manifest: "Those who love me will keep my word, and my Father will love them, and we will come to them and make our home with them" (Jn 14:23). Such a keeping of the Word leads the believer to become personally familiar with the divine mystery as intimately present.

SYMBOLS AND "THE SYMBOL"

Traditionally the creed has been called the *symbolum fidei*, the "symbol of faith." The common recitation of such a formula is, of course, a symbol of deeper lived unity. Still, there is another meaning to symbol. Literally it means "bringing things together," as opposed to the dia-bolic, "tearing things apart." In bringing the various articles together in this way, the symbol of faith expresses the special density of Christian belief. As an icon of the divine Word and Spirit, it points beyond its verbal form to the unity of all creation in Christ—to the unity lived in baptism and made possible in forgiveness, and offered in the one hope for the life to come. The divine mystery, the living Word, the sacrament of grace, and the totality of creation are brought together in the "symbol of faith." In that sense, the creed is deeply binding.

Further, in terming the creed the "symbol of faith," we are reminded of the broader sense in which the statements of faith are symbolic. The traditional word here is "analogical," that is, a referential kind of expression. We cannot speak of God or the things of God except by stretching the more usual range of human language to its limits. Not that this is a violent distortion: after all, there is only one universe of God's creation, of "all that is, seen and unseen." The visible and invisible are united in our human existence. To be human is to embody the unity of creation in a distinctive way. Hence, our knowing is marked by the relational, referential existence we are.

Further still, the divine has become human. Jesus, in the world of human beings, is revealed as the living expression of what God is: "Whoever has seen me has seen the Father" (Jn 14:9). Two incarnations—the human as embodying the material and spiritual dimensions of creation, and that of the Word become flesh amongst us—mark all our knowing with a symbolic, referential character. In the one creation, the incarnation of the Word, the images of the parables, the signs of the sacraments, the animated materiality of the body, and the embodied spirituality of the soul are each, in distinct but related ways, the foundation of analogical thinking.

Sometimes analogy is expressed in a simple metaphor, as when the creed asserts that Jesus Christ is "Light from Light," that "he came down from heaven," or "ascended into heaven," that he "is seated at the right hand of the Father." Sometimes the metaphor is more complex: the one God is "Father," "Son," and "Spirit" (literally "breath"), and is the "maker of heaven and earth"; Jesus is eternally "begotten of the Father," "through" him all things were made, he "became incarnate," he "rose again," he will "come" to judge the world; the Holy Spirit "has spoken through the Prophets" and there will be a "resurrection" of the dead. In each instance of such imaginative expressions, it takes some effort to be aware of what we are trying to say, and then to live with the frustration of not really being able to say it except in some referential sense. At the very least we tend to know what we don't mean, for such expressions are not to be taken in their usual everyday sense, as when we deal with ordinary realities. But these metaphors still point in a certain direction and work on a higher level of awareness to help focus on another order of reality—the ultimate, the transcendent, the divine.

Of course, sometimes the expression of the creed is starkly clear: "he was crucified under Pontius Pilate ... suffered death and was buried." There is no metaphor implied there. In contrast, the most difficult issues occur when we speak of God as "one," or as "maker" of all, when we refer to the Son as "of one Being" with the Father, or as "eternally" begotten, or to the "power" of the Holy Spirit. The point here is that the way God is one, or eternal, or creative, or simply *is*, remains a realm of total darkness for us. We can point from our human experience to something we know we must say, but just how such statements are verified with regard to God is outside of all human and created categories. Hence theologians usually say that what we affirm has to be followed by a kind of denial: for example, God is good, but *not* good in the merely limited ways of our direct experience of goodness. Our words pause tongue-tied before the limitless, unimaginable goodness of God. The mystery of God leaves all language silent and infinitely exceeds our capacities to express or grasp it. The fact that the Son, "of one Being with the Father," became man gives the infinite mystery a human face. In so doing, the incarnation heartens our expressions of faith with a special confidence and patience. Though the mystery cannot be yet fully revealed, it will be so in the end. Although an infinite gulf exists between God and our limited knowing, what God means by love is wonderfully confirming of what we mean by it: "for us ... and our salvation ..."

We note, too, that a certain oddness in the expression of the creed reminds us that it is the outcome of a particular history. It communicates to us over many hundreds of years from a long-past era. While the faith is the same, the tastes, sensibilities, priorities, problems, mind-set, and world-views vary from one generation to the next. Our faith is expressed in time, for God has time for the whole of human history. Even as we are joined to past generations in the recitation of this great creed, we still need to make it our own, in this time, in this world, in this language. Out of the ecumenical conversation now occurring around this classic creed, new possibilities for our own expressions of faith will emerge.

Still, the Nicene Creed has an essential value. It is a classic articulation of faith in the history of Christian self-expression. Its venerable antiquity enables us to reach back, through those sixteen hundred years, through countless baptisms and eucharists, through the confession of successive generations of believers, to those who found in the creed an enduring, focal expression of what they held to and wished to pass on. If this is how past believers put into words what they wished to hand on to us, our task, in a far distant age, is to make sense of it as best we can. The creed is part of our history. To neglect it, to leave it as a more or less unintelligible ritual expression, would be an odd kind of amnesia. Retrieving faith's past is the best resource for facing faith's future.

3
BELIEVERS

We/I believe in ...

Before moving into our examination of the body of the creed, we might pause on its first words. The opening phrase indicates those whose profession of faith it is—the "We" or "I" of the believers.

Who are these believers and what are they doing in their believing? While "We/I" are believing *in* God, it is *out of* a special experience of God in the hearts and minds and history of believers that the creed is expressed.

Given the hundreds of years of the scandal of Christian disunity and conflict, the very fact that at the present time we can find ourselves in this "We/I" of the creed is an indication of the grace of reconciliation at work. A more united "we" carries over into the later words, "for us ... and our salvation," to promise a new kind of inclusiveness. Grace has kept on being grace. Current reflections on the creed as a symbol of common faith are a powerful index of the Spirit at work. All Christians, in the presence of the one God, the one Lord, the one Holy Spirit, are being newly inspired to be the one Church.

Understandably there is plenty of room for argument about interpretation and emphasis. In the meantime, here *we* are. There is no point in moving to a consideration of the various articles of the creed unless we first look around at these others with whom we believe, and so look into ourselves in our believing: "... for those who do not love a brother or sister whom they have seen, cannot love God whom they have not seen" (1 Jn 4:20).

The "we," then, implies an open circle of fellow believers, in a state of reconciliation, in a mood of forgiveness, and in spiritual sympathy with all who continue to be "drawn by the Father" (Jn 6:44) to Christ. In the life of faith, individual believers and the community of believers are both linked with *you* in a journey into the fullness of life. The context is interpersonal and inclusive. There is no impersonal "it," no finally excluded "they," but a hopefully inclusive "we." Such personal communion is eroded by neither the death nor the succession of the generations. The "we" is ever increasing, extending beyond the grave to the "resurrection of the dead," to those who now see what we can only believe. The "we" of believers will be realized in "the life of the world to come."

Admittedly, the Latin and Greek versions of the creed, and their various translations, present an interesting question: How is the phrase "I believe" related to the expression "We believe"? The traditional Greek "we" (*pisteumonen*) resonates with the shared assurance of the early bishops gathered in councils and of the faithful sharing the reality of the eucharist. The Latin says "I" (*credo*), evoking the personal profession of faith in the newly baptized. Which is preferable?

In fact, faith demands both these polarities: there can be no "we" without individual commitments, and there is no "I" to believe without the prior "we" of the *sancta mater ecclesia*, Holy Mother Church. In both the individual and communal aspects of faith, believing is necessarily personal. Faith can only happen "in the first person." We don't get a free ride on an "it," however helpful the objective expression might be. Nor are we carried along by an anonymous body that does the believing for us. Whether it is "I" or "we" who do the believing, personal freedom and commitment are essential. There is no living off the faith of others, only living for and within it.

The creed exists to underscore the realism of the Gospel story uniting us in this moment of faith. Admittedly, it is possible for a non-believer to read the scriptures in a purely objective manner as "their story"—where "they" are the Jewish people or the early Christian communities. Such a reader might indeed marvel at how these human beings in the past came to have a common story which somehow included God in it—as the One who created the world and brought salvation through the course of history. In that sense, the Bible would offer the elements of both a human and a divine biography, as it tells how these people came to have a common history, and how God was identified and invoked within it.

With faith, a new field of meaning occurs. "Their" story becomes "our/my" story. And the story of God comes to be told more in terms of a divine autobiography including the actual life-stories of all who come to believe: "This is my Son, the Beloved ... listen to him!" (Mt 17:5). It is a communication from heart to heart. Paul could situate himself in the divine story by confessing, "[He] loved me and gave himself for me" (Gal 2:20). For John, the Word becomes flesh, to become a promise: "We will come to them and make our home with them"(Jn 14:23). God dwells in the hearts of those who believe. The incarnate Word also becomes a prayer: "that they may be one, as we are one ..."(Jn 17:22). In such a promise and through such a prayer, faith reads a divine autobiography written in the Word expressed in Jesus Christ.

In the meaning of that Word, the "I" and the "we" of faith finds its most complete identity. Let us dwell for a moment on each polarity, first accenting the "I," and then the "we."

"I BELIEVE"

On an elemental level, human consciousness is embedded in the physical, chemical, and biological processes of the world. As so embodied, we are affected by the push and pull inherent in the fact that we are immersed in the all-encompassing happening of the universe.

If we are not to drown in a flux of instincts and impressions and needs, consciousness must expand. We lift our heads out of the water, to ask what it all means. Various dimensions of meaning enable us to position ourselves within a world of past, present, and future, of near and far, of science, art, and human learning in all its forms. In short, we learn to speak a language, and, in a sense, the language speaks us. Words form our consciousness just as that consciousness is clarified, supported, and communicated by words.

Yet it would be a peculiarly weightless world if that awareness of meaningfulness and our capacities to speak remained unbeholden to the truth of things. To be concerned for truth is to be prepared to probe beyond mere bright ideas, or imaginative insights, beyond just what is meaningful to me, to what is in fact the case for all. Consciousness is charged with personal gravity in the measure we are beholden to the truth, and so enabled to appear before one another as trustworthy, reliable speakers of that truth in the great conversation of human history.

Then, the more deeply we are rooted in the good ground of reality, the more we begin to feel the attraction of values—not merely as noble feelings, but as a fundamental orientation of our lives. Alive to such values, we are present to one another as honest, cooperative, generously hospitable to the demands of a shared good, and eager and able to implement it.

Consciousness expands—upward and outward. It ejects us from merely drifting with the flux of things to make each of us a partner in the conversation about life's meaning. It enables us to stand before others as tellers of truth and to journey with them as doers of the good. With all people of good will we stand within the totality of life's mystery, to share with them the force of such questions as: What is the meaning of all our meanings? What is the ultimate reason for everything we find true? What is the ultimate good in everything we find worthwhile?

When the gift of faith occurs, it intimates an all-fulfilling answer to the elemental questions making up our conscious life. A limitless love now supports and invites the upward and outward movement of human life.

Faith, from this point of view, is our highest and deepest sense of reality, as it connects us, however unobtrusively, with the creative presence of God. For the "I" of the believer is now conscious of itself as "drawn by the Father," attracted by a limitless love promising life's fullness and completion. The world of our many meanings is brought together in the light of the

Word, the Light from Light, Meaning incarnate among us: "Through him all things were made." The energies of our freedom are now empowered by God's indwelling Spirit. Faith comes to know the holiness that heals, makes whole, and promises hope — "the Spirit, the Lord, the giver of life."

In effect, what enables each one to say "I believe" and mean it is the gift that confirms and illumines the fundamental outgoing, relational movement of our conscious lives. The believing "I" is a self aware of its limitless openness. To live now means to be drawn out of ourselves in self-surrender and adoration.

This "I" is graced, the recipient of God's limitless gift. It is the "I" who has been drawn by the Father to Christ (Jn 6:44), who is loved by God and becomes the dwelling of the Father and the Son (Jn 14:23). Paul, in a highly personal statement that can still be applied generally (Gal 2:19–20), can declare that as a believer he has been "crucified with Christ" so that "it is no longer I who live, but it is Christ who lives in me." In the tensions and ambiguities of living in the "flesh" of this earthly life, the apostle's deepest life is governed by faith in the one "who loved me and gave himself for me." The individuality of faith is further enhanced in that "To each is given the manifestation of the Spirit for the common good" (1 Cor 12:7). In the realm of God's action in our lives, each of us is given to the other, and to all, as a gift.

In that the "drawing," "indwelling," by being united to the Crucified, and loved by him, and in being gifted with a unique spiritual "manifestation," each of us utters the "I" of the creed. Each believer gives meaning to the personal pronoun out of the unique grace and calling he or she has received.

The self realised in faith is not contained in the varieties of scripts and roles and identities that our culture and society impose. All of these, provisionally necessary though they might be, are ultimately depressing if they demand a total self-investment. For the whole expansive God-defined reality of what I am is reduced to something infinitely less—or to someone telling me who I am and what I should be and do. In contrast, there is a certain element of joyous abandon in the relational consciousness of the believer. With the gift of faith, the human person refuses to be defined by anything save the infinite mystery, the homeland of our hearts. Only in that reality is the fullness of identity to be found:

> Beloved, we are God's children now; what we will be has
> not yet been revealed. What we do know is this: when
> he is revealed, we will be like him, for we will see him as
> he is. (1 Jn 3:2)

The "I" of the believer is present to itself in a kind of elemental passion. By believing, I am refusing to settle for anything less than life to the full. I anticipate, however implicitly, a final judgment when the true reality of God and creation will be revealed, when the promise of our humanity will finally be kept. To believe is to rest ill-content with anything less than total salvation, for oneself and for others.

This is not to imply that the believing self is all at once complete in a single confession of faith. Nonetheless, the movement has begun. The believer in question is now in touch with inexhaustible principles of renewal and conversion. There can be no limit to one's surrender to God, and to the wholeness of mind and heart and soul and strength found in loving the one who has first loved us. There is, further, no limit to our exploration of the mysteries to which the creed invites us. Because the creed is a limited human language, the believer is always in a state of being converted through an ongoing process of learning and dialogue on faith's meaning. Most importantly, values that were hitherto unfelt or unnoticed begin to emerge as fresh demands on the believer's integrity. The moral world of ecology, social justice, sexual relationships, economic responsibility and scientific detachment invite us into a limitless challenge of the good to be done. Though such imperatives may often leave the believer defeated and defensive, the summons to something more does not cease; and the way forward is in deeper humility and trust. Faith must work itself out in love if the great mysteries we confess are to be real in our world and in our lives, if I am finally to find myself in the Light: "Now I know only in part; then I will know fully, even as I have been fully known" (1 Cor 13:12).

"WE BELIEVE"

But now let us turn to the other polarity, the "we" in which every believing "I" is connected to the past, incorporated in the present, and directed to the future. The words of the creed are not a private language. They express a shared identity and a living communication.

It has been often remarked that all knowledge and art is deeply convivial. It lives from a celebratory sense of the achievements of others. The most brilliant scientist or the most inspired artist comes to an outstanding achievement only within a community of shared experience and in reliance on the gradual accumulation of a solidly tested sense of reality. Such is also the case in the "We believe" of faith. It is possible only in the conviviality of liturgy, of a common recognition of the inspired scriptures, of communicating with common symbols, of sharing the common burden and grace of mission, in all the ways we pray and ponder, speak, and work together.

The creed is not an expression of some kind of spiritual capitalism. It does not prescribe a development of what I own apart from or to the exclusion of others. In the presence of the Source of all gifts, we are not spiritual entrepreneurs. Nor for that matter are we simply religious socialists, in the sense of having no identity save in the collective of the believing community. The breakdown of notions of capitalist individualism and socialist collectivism that has occurred this century is an opportunity to recover and enhance a deeper sense of "I" and "we," and how they are related. We come before God neither as a collection of individual self-seeking egos, nor in the anonymity of the mass of believers.

This is to say that our existence in God is relational. We share in the communal character of the trinitarian life. Even the divine persons are each what they are only from and for the others. The Father, however almighty we might confess him to be, is only Father as related to the Son and the Spirit. The Trinity is a communion of love and life. As we are drawn into that communion, we each become a member of Christ, a temple of the Holy Spirit, a son/daughter of the Father. Believing means living in the midst of such relationships, dwelling in them, caught up in them, implementing them in the humble domain of our existence in the daily life of this planet.

Any appreciation of the "we" who believe recognises not only the prior "we" of the divine persons, but the historical "we" of the church bringing us forth in the life of faith, to give us this language of shared identity. The "I believe" is set within the "we" of apostles, martyrs, prophets, saints, mystics, confessors, teachers, pastors, founders, and reformers. The existence of the prior engendering "we" is classically expressed in the opening words of John's letter:

> We declare to you what was from the beginning, what
> we have heard, what we have seen with our eyes, what
> we have looked at and touched with our hands,
> concerning the word of life—this life was revealed, and
> we have seen it and testify to it, and declare to you the
> eternal life that was with the Father and was revealed to
> us—we declare to you what we have seen and heard so
> that you also may have fellowship with us; and truly our
> fellowship is with the Father and with his Son Jesus
> Christ. We are writing these things so that our joy may
> be complete. (1 Jn 1:1–4)

To that degree the "We believe" of today completes the joyous assurance of those original witnesses, and of those who have transmitted life's most precious meaning to us at this moment of time. The community of faith continues to be shaped within the accumulated belief of past generations—it lives from the *depositum fidei*, the riches of living tradition. And each generation of faith enriches the common fund of Christian experience and tradition. For the influence of past believers is not a dead weight, but a creative resource out of which the distinctive "I believe" of each believer is shaped. Each believer lives for, and dies into, a larger communication stretching into the future as a grace for generations yet to come. The "complete joy" of faith is possessed as looking forward to the full number of those who will come to believe.

4

BELIEVING

We *believe in ...*

What does "believing" mean in these opening words of the creed? It implies the activity and attitude of those who are in contact with God. God loves, God gives, God reveals: as a result, we believe. Believing, then, is an inspired openness to God's self-giving love: "Now faith is the assurance of things hoped for, the conviction of things not seen" (Heb 11:1). Faith must consist in a relationship to God as simple and as complex as the whole field of our existence in this present life.

If simplicity remains the ideal—to relate to God with whole heart and mind and soul and strength—complexity is the problem. To exist is to teeter on the brink of an immense reality that we can never fully grasp. We either hold on or fall down: "If you do not stand firm in faith, you shall not stand at all" (Isa 7:9). In the original Hebrew of these words, a kind of pun on the root word *amn* (from which "amen" derives) is implied. It can mean both "believing" and, more literally, "standing."

Another interesting root: the Latin *credere* is thought to mean *cor dare*, "to give one's heart"—thus resonating with the biblical injunction to love God "with all one's heart."

Given the intensity of the biblical and theological meaning of believing, the modern meaning of "belief" is much thinner and indeterminate. For instance, there is the strong "I believe in you," and the rather less consequential "I believe in having a good

33

breakfast." Then, again, there is the implication of mere hearsay, as in "I believe it was raining in Sydney yesterday." Or, to take another interesting example, "I believe only good things about you"—as though believing in this instance means screening out a range of more compromising data, with the implication, "I believe you though thousands wouldn't!"

Again, in the weak sense of current language, there is the "seeing is believing" type of idiom. The implication is that the only real knowing is seeing with one's own eyes, while believing is merely a secondhand and derivative affair. So, the many possible resonances of the verb "to believe" point to the need to probe the biblical and theological usage more carefully. Here a number of points can be made.

First of all, believing, as the creed uses the word, means affirming the truth. It has a defiant edge to it. In the ambiguities and defeats of our history, believing is a decisive affirmative activity. It takes its stand on the divine reality, which is never reducible to an intra-worldly element or factor, and which is disclosed only in the vulnerability and beauty of self-giving love. More generally, to believe means, despite all temptations to doubt and apathy, to recognize the value and meaning in the heart of existence. It counters our arrogant propensity to be full of ourselves, to direct us, in humility, to where the true fullness of reality is to be found.

As a kind of affirmative action on behalf of the true meaning of life, believing means self-surrender to mystery that has revealed itself. While not denying the existence of difficulties, obscurities, ambiguities and scandals, faith makes its stand in the midst of all such confusion. Such believing feels like a risk. It means throwing in our lot with God (and with our fellow believers) in the great experiment of Christian faith: "And this is the victory that conquers the world, our faith" (1 Jn 5:4).

Such an approach might make believing sound too gullible or vulnerable, as though our intelligence had to be sacrificed to some kind of infantile credulity. But there is another side to believing. Nothing happens in life or knowledge or art unless there is some basic trust at the heart of our search. Even modern literary figures like Sartre who maintain the utter absurdity of reality are practicing a kind of belief. They are making an affirmation that cannot be proved, and indeed, one which seems to involve a self-contradiction as they give reasons why absurdity must prevail!

Though there is a feeling of risk involved in the life of faith, to hang back waiting to prove everything before taking a step would make living impossible. Without a prior surrender to the whole as meaningful and good, doubts would be too many, scandals too great, and anxiety too pervasive for anyone to act.

Still, we do have the problem of the extremely open connotations today of our English word "believe." The biblical and doctrinal tradition needs a stronger carrier if the full Christian meaning of faith is to be understood. It has often been pointed out that "believe" once had a much stronger meaning in English, somewhat akin to "be-love." If there was a verbal form of "faith" such as "faith-ing" (as in biblical Greek, though not in Latin), we could translate "we believe" as "we 'faith' in God," which might be closer to the point. Still, we have to work with the language we presently have. More realistically, we might get to the meaning by distinguishing, but not separating, the two notions "faith" and "belief," to bring them together in the fundamental activity of affirming God as giver and goal of true life.

Here, an interesting and influential distinction in the Latin vocabulary of faith, originally made by St Augustine, emerges in the history of theology: *credere **in Deum*** (to believe IN God), *credere **Deum*** (to believe THAT God is ...), *credere **Deo*** (to believe BY God).

Believing IN God (*in Deum*) is religious faith enabling the believer to "indwell" the divine reality with a kind of inside knowledge of God.

On the other hand, believing THAT God is, that God is loving, merciful, etc., unpacks that fundamental relationship into human words and judgments. It amounts to expressing our belief in doctrinal statements *about* God. However, without the first form of believing, confessing anything "about God" could be merely external, or merely cultural, without any interior engagement of the heart—as in the faith of the demons in the Gospels!

Then there is BY God (*Deo*). The implication here is that we believe "on divine authority," through the witness of God's Word and Spirit and as "drawn by the Father"; our ability to indwell the divine reality is a God-given grace. Faith is a gift.

Clearly, as a verbal formula, the creed is about God: a set of statements. Thereby it expresses a meaning which, in principle, anyone can study and analyse. In the present context of theological and spiritual reflection, we are assuming that the act of believing and the expression of our common faith is a much more intimate affair—as the three aspects of believing outlined above suggest. In order to clarify this further, we shall pause on two notions, "faith" and "belief."

FAITH

First of all, faith. Faith in God is an unreserved surrender to God by divine grace. Through a union with God that only the Spirit of love can give, the person of faith dwells not only in the divine mystery, but in the whole reality of creation in a new way. The whole, the "all," is experienced as a universe of grace. All that is, "seen and unseen," is comprehended by the "almighty" love of the Father, just as through the beloved Son "all things were made." An all-encompassing love reaches into the darkest depths of human existence: "for our sake, he was crucified ... ; he suffered death and was buried." Such an experience of the totality implies a sense of the universe moving toward an ultimate completion: "the resurrection of the dead, and the life of the world to come."

All in all, faith is a consciousness of the abundant life (Jn 10:10) pulsing through the universe, which is communicated to the believer through the "giver of life," the Spirit of Christ. In its radical self-surrender, faith lives from the truth that will "make you free" (Jn 8:32)—free from anxieties of guilt and cosmic despair ("the forgiveness of sins"), free for a life of communion with the divine ("the resurrection ... the life of the world to come"). St Thomas Aquinas states that faith is not a matter of accepting divinely legitimated propositions, but of actually attaining the divine reality itself: "The act of the believer does not terminate at the statement, but at a *reality*" (*Summa Theol.*, 2–2, 1, 2 ad 2).

Further, the consciousness of faith, in its holistic sense of God in all and all in God, is alive with a joy that "no one will take ... from you" (Jn 16:22; cf. 15:11). The sadness of death, failure, disease, suffering, and guilt does not have the last word. It is a consciousness of the "peace which the world cannot give" (Jn 14:27, *New Jerusalem Bible*), a state of assurance beyond the confusions of our endlessly complex existence. It is a consciousness that blossoms in the conviction that nothing in all creation can separate us from the love of God in Christ Jesus (Rom 8:37–39).

The consciousness of faith, then, is human awareness expanding to a certain peak of fulfillment. The believer has undergone a conversion to reach that turning point where God is the really real and the ultimately loving. The special level of consciousness that faith occupies can be "broadened and deepened and heightened and enriched," but it cannot be outgrown or transcended by some other demand. It is living at the point of loving and being loved.* Faith yields only to the direct vision of God in "the world to come."

The first letter of Peter captures the ultimate poise of faith in a beautiful declaration:

> Although you have not seen him, you love him; and even
> though you do not see him now, you believe in him and
> rejoice with an indescribable and glorious joy, for you
> are receiving the outcome of your faith, the salvation of
> your souls. (1 Pet 1:8–9)

In this sense, faith is the soul of the creed. Without it, any formula of faith would be empty.

BELIEFS

On the other hand, faith does find expression in a world of words and meanings. It is articulated in the midst of all the variety of ways human beings believe. Unless faith is "worded" in some way,

---

* Bernard J. F. Lonergan, S. J., *Method in Theology*, Darton, Longman & Todd, London, 1972, p. 107.

it would be simply an adoring silence. However desirable this might be in its place, however strong a witness contemplative silence can be in a world of empty chatter, faith would be disembodied if it did not busy itself to find the best words to express, however imperfectly, the reality it lived. Because the Word became flesh, faith cannot stand apart from the great conversation that makes up human history. Because it has something supremely worth saying, it has to learn the vocabulary in which to say, with proper precision, Yes or No; or to make a qualified judgment, as when it comes to see that this expression is better than that. Without expressing itself in a body of beliefs, the life of faith would be a secret, kept from the world for which it is meant.

By the very fact and, indeed, in the very act of indwelling the mystery of God, faith is continually provoked into finding the best words in which to express itself. It must become articulate in the world of human meaning. The way faith has faced such a challenge has a long history. Different languages, cultures, societies, and epochs demand of Christian believers to say what they mean. As a result, we have the scriptures, the documents of tradition, doctrines, moral commandments, theologies, art, all the variety of Christian witness—and the creeds themselves.

As faith expresses itself in a variety of beliefs, they, in turn, embody, protect, and form faith. In the historical community of believers, new generations of believers have to be instructed. Older generations have to be directed, encouraged, and supported in new situations.

It is well to note that the expression and acceptance of beliefs are not an especially religious phenomenon. So much of human life is a matter of believing and of depending on the word of others. Even the most abstruse mathematical formulae have to rely on principles that cannot be verified within their formulations, as Kurt Gödel has demonstrated. If we insisted on having immediate knowledge of everything that affected us, we could hardly live at all. For example, you can use a computer without having any special knowledge of its inner workings. As you write or compute, you are believing, relying on hundreds of others who through millions of work hours have achieved the electronic and mechanical expertise to make the machine and design the programs you now use. Similarly, if you are traveling, you rely on maps that others have made, to find your way around new territory.

Further, in a major way, each culture is a great pattern of beliefs. Simply by breathing its air, its members are inclined to believe this way or that. When a culture is more religious, atheists are regarded as an oddity. If, however, it is atheistic, as in the Marxist Soviet republics of recent times, religious believers are victimized as subversive or benighted. Today, in more pluralist times, with the influence of mass media, people often express the quandary of not knowing who or what to believe. The man or woman of proven competence in some area can at such times have an almost disproportionate influence. So a leading scientist can pass judgment on matters of religion without having any special familiarity with the realities under discussion, as once a religious leader could sway the faithful to accept technical or political positions without any special expertise in those areas. But the fact remains that we have to believe if we are to understand, not only in religious instances but in human knowledge generally.

Christian belief, then, functions in a world of believing. Whether it is a better way of believing in contrast to other ways, how it is related to other cultural beliefs and in what way it supports or contradicts them, is each a matter of endless theological discussion.

Our Christian beliefs indicate something of the apostolicity of Church. The Gospel and its faith have to be incarnated in time and culture. Unless there were a Christian institution with express beliefs, unless faith were worded and shaped in history with authority and clarity, our Christian presence in the world would remain inarticulate. Beliefs form the faith into a definite meaning.

It may seem a little crass to liken the creed, as a classic expression of Christian belief, to a computer program or a map, as we did above. But there is a similarity. For the creed draws us into a history of the spiritual maps and images of what has made sense to generations of past believers. We are formed by their words and directed by their judgments. We live from the testimony and teaching of those who, in their lives and deaths, have witnessed to the reality of the risen One. Their pattern of belief is programmed into our present faith.

It is, of course, possible that beliefs can be mistaken or confused. There can be a virus in the computer and maps can lead to dead ends. But, in general, the proof is in the pudding. The truth will be revealed, and we will learn, sadder and wiser, who and what we should trust. Believing is self-correcting; the maps become more refined; the computer can be protected against viruses; a better, more refined articulation of faith can be achieved ...

In this regard, the creed actually is a record of learning. The community of Christian faith had to formulate its judgments in reaction to a variety of false or confusing beliefs that tended to undermine the integrity of faith. Though these false beliefs are not expressly stated in the creed, they have influenced its expression. For example: God is the creator of everything, visible and invisible—not just of the spiritual world (against the Manichees); Jesus is eternally begotten of the Father—not merely created in time (against Arius); Jesus was truly human, died, and was buried—not just apparently a man (against the Docetists); the Holy Spirit is Lord with the Father and the Son—not just an energizing activity of God in some impersonal way (against those denying the divinity of the Holy Spirit); Jesus rose "in accordance with the Scriptures," and the Holy Spirit spoke through the prophets—against any implication that the God of Israel was some other kind of God (against Marcion); the one God is Father, Son, and Spirit—against interpreting the divine three as phases or modes of divine revelation (against Modalism). Even though other points might be added, these just mentioned are at least an indication of how the creed is a compendium of right beliefs and the outcome of an experience of learning how faith needed right formulation.

And such learning must go on. Communicating the Gospel to all nations and epochs can never allow the Church to be satisfied that it has achieved the most perfect and persuasive expression of its teaching and beliefs. To give one instance, note how our creed mentions nothing about the life of Jesus—simply that he became man and was crucified. Modern writers of creeds would no doubt be inspired to say more about his actual humanity—his solidarity with the poor, the parables of the Kingdom, the morality of the Beatitudes and the New Commandment, and the sacraments of baptism and eucharist. Further, in a world of intense inter-faith dialogue and concern, the implication that the "for us ... and our salvation" must be worked out in regard to God willing "everyone to be saved and to come to the knowledge of the truth" (1 Tim 2:4). In other words, as the understanding of faith increases, as different cultures and mentalities offer their various challenges, and as conversion intensifies, new formulations of faith become possible and desirable. It is not only a matter of breathing new life into ancient formulations. The expression of Christian belief develops within history.

FOUR DIMENSIONS OF FAITH'S MEANING

Yet as an expression of meaning, beliefs work in different ways. Most obviously, believing in Christ affirms some quite definite realities in a quite objective manner. In short, beliefs aim to confess the truth: the real God is revealed in Christ—and the divine reality is as Christ reveals it. Beliefs are focused in what is called a *cognitive* meaning. They express the judgment of faith, saying Yes when it means Yes, and No when it means No, just as they confess that *this*, not *that*, is the case. Authentic beliefs orientate the believer in a universe of truth.

Then, there is another range of meaning. By believing in the triune God, believers indwell, and are indwelt by, the divine mystery in such a way that they are given a new sense of identity. The objectivity of faith gives us a new subjectivity, a new self involved in the activity of faith. We relate to God in the intimacy of being sons and daughters of the Father because we are all inter-related as members of the one Body of Christ, and vitalized by the indwelling Spirit. The creed, to speak technically, is thus *constitutive* of Christian identity. By affirming who God is, it tells us who we are.

Thirdly, by believing in the divine reality, and having this new identity because of it, we relate to one another in a new way.

Beliefs are shared. They form believers into a community of faith, and enhance that community by articulating common meanings and values. Current ecumenical interest in the Nicene Creed bears this out. From this point of view, beliefs articulate *communicative* meaning.

Fourthly, beliefs inspire us to act in a certain way. They have an *effective* meaning. As we believe in God in this way, as we dwell in such truth, and find both identity and community in the saving mystery, we are inspired to act in a certain way. In glorifying the Holy Spirit with the Father and the Son, in looking to the "resurrection of the dead" and the "life of the world to come," the creed as a privileged expression of belief demands that we begin to live now in a manner anticipating our future in God. Hence, Christian action must participate in God's saving love; we must love as Christ loves, and be merciful as our heavenly Father is merciful, to bear the fruit of the Spirit in peace and justice, and in resistance to the ungracious powers that diminish and distort the good world of God's creation in Christ. In this way, beliefs promote a present transformation of life in the light of the world to come.

As faith and its living body of beliefs enter into the great human conversation, Christian meaning unfolds in the four ways I mention. A Christian truth is affirmed; a Christian identity is named; a Christian community is formed; a Christian way of life is inspired. This is a complex process, not only because of the variety of challenges that history keeps presenting, but, most radically, because the mystery of God can never be exhausted. Believing is our way of allowing for the fullness of God's saving grace to be revealed in its own time and in its own terms: "Blessed are those who have not seen and yet have come to believe" (Jn 20:29).

5

THE MYSTERY OF GOD

<hr>

... one God,
the Father, the Almighty,
maker of heaven and earth,
of all that is, seen and unseen.

The first article of the creed introduces the unique, limitless originality of the love that creates, gives itself, and redeems. We believe in God by dwelling in the One in whom "we live and move and have our being" (Acts 17:28). The reality of God is the milieu of our existence. The infinite and eternal has come near, to enfold us into its own life.

As with all the other articles of the creed, we are faced with what cannot be fully known within the limits of human knowledge: "No one has ever seen God" (Jn 1:18). Only by faith in Christ do we become personally familiar with the mystery: "It is God the only Son, who is close to the Father's heart, who has made him known (Jn 1:18). The Word incarnate reveals the human face of God. Only the Spirit enables us to hear the full reality of the Word that could not be borne except in faith (Jn 16:12–14). In this one divine truth, the faith of Israel and the faith of the Church are united:

Hear, O Israel: the Lord our God, the Lord is one; you shall love the Lord your God with all your heart, and with all your soul, and with all your mind, and with all your strength. (Mk 12:29–30; cf. Deut 6:4–5; Mt 22:37; Lk 10:27)

43

God is thus the one to be loved with all the best energies of our being, in all our powers to know, to feel, to act, and to relate. In this One alone do our hearts find rest and our souls reach their salvation. In this One our minds adore the all-surpassing truth that summons them, and our actions find their scope and fulfillment.

In adoring, loving, and entrusting ourselves to this One, we belong together most fully as "we," and enter a community of love and forgiveness. For the commandment following the summons to love God wholly is "You shall love your neighbor as yourself" (Mk 12:31).

All our capacities to transcend this world, to become more than the limited versions of our social and cultural identities, and to follow the instinct and summons of true life, find their point of rest in the one God: "For with you is the fountain of life; in your light we see light" (Ps 36:9).

Yet, to enter into the mystery of the one God, we do not lose ourselves in an infinite solitude. For this One does not live in transcendent isolation, but in the vitality of infinite interpersonal love. God is communication: Father, Son, and Spirit, the source of the unity of the "one holy Church" and of "the life of the world to come."

The one God is a unity-in-communion enfolding believers into itself, that they may dwell in, and live by, a divine vitality:

The glory that you have given me I have given them, so
that they may be one, as we are one, I in them and you in
me, that they may become completely one. (Jn 17:22–23)

This One alone is adored as God. The great reality beckons at once within, yet beyond, the time-and-space-bound limits of human existence. God acts so that human beings search for their ultimate fulfillment; it is not the other way round, as if our searching discovers God and somehow stimulates divine grace to act. Paul, in his discourse to the Athenians, emphasizes the divine initiative:

... he allotted the times of their existence and the
boundaries of [their] places ... so that they would search

for God and perhaps grope for him and find him—
though indeed he is not far from each one of us. For "In
him we live and move and have our being" ... (Acts
17:26–28)

Given the atheism or idolatries of our day, faith in the one
God is a counter-cultural stance. Biblically speaking, faith in the
one true God is always a choice against more obvious cultural
deities—the "false gods"—whatever they might be: "You shall
have no other gods before me" (Deut 5:7). God is neither the
deification of nature (Baal; cf. 1 Kings 16–18), nor the idolization
of political power (Moloch; cf. Lev 18–20, 1 Kings 11:7) or of
possessions (Mammon; cf. Mt 6:24, etc.)—we cannot serve both
the one God and false gods. In the end, idols inspire not the
freeing and fulfilling self-surrender of faith, but the sacrifice of
what is most graciously human within us.

Believing in the one God is, then, an act of cultural defiance.
In contesting all forms of cultural self-enclosure, faith is an
enduring source of creativity within history and society. In the
face of the emptiness and universal doubt that greatly affect the
modern era, faith in the one God is a foundation of new hope.
Distinctive features of our modern epoch are the loss of a sense of
the transcendent and a prevailing cosmic despair. For the first time
in world history, the existence of God is no longer presumed in the
public, social, intellectual, and moral conversation of the times.

Yet there are possibilities in the new situation that are to be
welcomed. In the harsh criticisms of atheism, the creed is led back
to its true character as an act of faith. Believers are no longer
offered a free ride on general forms of cultural religiosity. The
"masters of suspicion" have rightly unmasked conventional
religiosity as a human projection and social subterfuge. If Marx
undermined religious belief as an ideology of privilege, faith in
the true God sets believers in solidarity with the poor of the
world. If Freud unmasked religion as infantile projection, a new
adult faith can allow its spirituality to be a force for freedom. If
science was intent on replacing the God of faith with what can be
measured, controlled, and analysed, a purified faith can lead back

all knowledge to reveal the original character of the universe as God's creation. If Nietzsche bitterly reproached Christianity as a resentful belittling of humanity, a newly humanized faith can find in God a foundation for a new inclusive co-humanity of responsibility and mutual service.

"God" as an idol has been toppled, along with the gods of the group, of psychological projection, and of social security—the many gods of human presumption and consumption.

While faith draws us into its own world of images, it presents them precisely as images, as icons, not as idols or as mere fabrications of human sentiment. As icons, the images of faith are designed to let the mystery come on its own terms. Faith is indeed illumined in the light of scripture, the Church, the sacraments, doctrines, and Christ himself. All these contain elements of creative human expression. Still, they are not merely the products of human creativity. A deeper inspiration is at work. The images of faith shine with a light from beyond them; they bespeak the infinity of the mystery that has expressed itself in our world. The symbols of faith are not projected onto the blank screen of human aspiration, but back-lit, as it were, by the revelation of a love not of this world.

In such light, faith lets God be God, in the scandal and folly of the Crucified, in a humble invocation of the Spirit, in the shared celebration and witness of God's people, those who believe ...

A purified faith allows for the re-appearance of God in the post-religious, godless world. The myth, not the science, of evolution tended to undermine human dignity and the world itself as God's creation. Yet as naive notions of how God acts in nature are surpassed, faith can explore how God is ever creative, as the great attractor drawing the immense, groaning, manifold totality of the cosmos towards its goal.

The gracious riddle of Israel's invocation of the Lord as YHWH, the One who gave his name as "I will be who I will be" (cf. Ex 3:14), has led the generations of faith to this God who is now self-revealed in Christ and the Spirit. However unreserved that communication, it can only be received in faith and fulfilled in the life of the world to come. The words of faith are spoken in a great silence, provoking a listening and attentive searching for words to serve the truth, not to contain or constrict it, nor to reduce it to anything less than the One who is. Every believer knows something of Elijah's heart. Though, with the prophet, we can defy the false gods, the true God is finally known only in humble self-surrender to that "sound of sheer silence" (1 Kings 19:12), the space of mystery in which the whole world groans for fulfillment.

In this way, God is indeed "no-thingness"—not like anything else contained within the horizon of our knowing, within the reference of our words, within the glimmer of our ideas and concepts. Gregory of Nyssa, one of the great mystical doctors of the Church, wrote:

> The unlimited divine nature cannot be accurately
> contained by a name. Rather, every capacity for concepts
> and every form of words and names, even if they seem to
> contain something great and befitting God's glory, are
> unable to grasp God's reality. But starting from certain
> traces and sparks, as it were, our words aim at the
> unknown, and from what we grasp we make conjectures
> by a kind of analogy of the ungraspable.*

However intimately present to the heart of faith, this one God infinitely exceeds anything else we know.

Our speech about God is always analogical language as it shuffles between what is known in our experience and what is unknown in the divine reality itself. Words unfold into an all-meaningful silence. Provisional clarity eventually leads to darkness. In comparison with the defined and limited realities of our world, God is "no-thing." God is not contained within any category or concept or model. Even as the creed affirms the saving reality of God, it does not encapsulate it. It forms our faith and belief to await the transformation that only God can give, not as a sublime idea but as the living, acting presence that makes all the difference.

* Gregory of Nyssa, *Commentary on the Song of Songs*, Chapter 1, v. 3, C. McCambley (trans.), Hellenic College Press, Brookline Mass., 1987, p. 53.

Little wonder that some imaginative religious writers try to re-introduce a wholesome reverence into our speech about God with such verbal signals as "G—d." Believers must not talk God to death. The mystery does not encourage us to engage in religious chatter, but to speak the committed words of faith in prayerful adoration, only when our hearts are right and intent on loving: "Beloved, let us love one another, because love is from God; everyone who loves is born of God and knows God ... for God is love" (1 Jn 4:7–8). We are plunged into the reality of a life we can never objectify or stand back from. To exist, to live, finally to love, is to be caught up in a homeland of mystery more real than the air we breathe.

The primary stance of committed faith is not that of having to prove the existence of God. Rather, the opposite. Believers are more intent on proving, not God's existence, but the genuineness of their own existence as responsive to the mystery into which they are drawn. It is less a matter of proving the existence of God, more a challenge to affirm the divine mystery as the central reality of our existence.

Still, to believe is not to become intellectually paralyzed. Faith is not isolated from the intellectual or moral concerns of life. It is to be lived not as stupidity, but as an integrating wisdom.

Consequently, in its experience of the divine, Christian tradition does recognize proofs or arguments for God's existence. Perhaps the word "proof" is far too cut and dried. It suggests that the existence of God can be established as one more fact, pinned down by rational control as one factor among many within a philosophic or scientific system. But God is outside any system, and beyond any thought. Proof, in such a naive, superficial, and logical sense, cannot conclude as to the reality of what Christians speak of as "God."

Even "arguing" to God's existence, while more modest in its connotation, still perhaps is all too heady for the searching and groping spoken of by Paul (Acts 17:27).

Perhaps "intimation" is better. The word suggests something of heart and mind moving together to what must remain beyond our grasp, even if "not far from each one of us." It connotes both

God's action—intimation in an active sense—and our experience of it—intimation in a passive sense. We cannot evade questions arising out of the depths of what and who we are in this world. Such questions are posed in the intimacy of our living consciousness as it expands through all the relationships that make up our lives. When life is fired at us pointblank, the uncanny fact of the sheer existence of the universe and of ourselves within it demands exploration.

Thus, we can be part of the time-honored exercise of attempting to give reasons why "God" can mean what faith, in fact, already lives. As faith expands its capacities to reflect and understand, it can include, as it were, an appreciation of the universe as God's creation. The more believers gather to themselves the intelligibility of the universe, the more realistic is their cosmic praise:

> Bless the Lord, all you works of the Lord;
> sing praise to him and highly exalt him forever.
> (Dan 3:57)

Traditionally, such intimations of God's existence were based on the objective inexplicability of the world on its own terms. For instance, there had to be a first cause since no one element of reality, nor all of it together, is a sufficient explanation of why anything exists, nor of why the universe has emerged the astonishing way it has. True, this is not so much "proving the existence" of God, as arguing that the world is ultimately not self-explanatory. Intelligence must look for an ultimate explanation and ask why any such explanation is truly ultimate, that is, does not presuppose anything else.

Of course, in recent times this line of argument has been taken further as the billions of years of cosmic time have been gradually explored through a series of astonishing discoveries: the Big Bang, the formation of the galaxies and of the earth, the emergence of life, and the manner in which the universe is aware of itself in the consciousness of the human mind and heart. The wonder-filled event of our universe has made science itself remarkably open-minded on the possibility of an original, provident, and limitless Mind behind it all. After the pondering of such possibilities, an outstanding modern philosopher suggests some fascinating questions facing the modern thinker:

> ... to speculate creatively and imaginatively as to what the "personality" or "character" must be like of a Creator in whose image this astonishing universe of ours is made, with its prodigal abundance of energy, its mind-boggling complexity yet simplicity, its fecundity of creative spontaneity, its ever surprising fluid interweaving of order and chance, law and apparent chaos, and so forth. Must not the personality of such a Creator be charged not only with unfathomable wisdom, power and exuberant generosity, but also with dazzling "imaginative" creativity—might we say a daring Cosmic Gambler who delights in working out his providence by a creative synthesis of both law and order, on the one hand, and chance, risk, spontaneity, on the other—a "coincidence of opposites" as St Bonaventure put it long ago?*

To believe in God does not exclude believers from the conversation that makes up human culture. They share in the adventure of intelligence and wonder, to insist that the ultimate question be raised, and to offer a special kind of data—and even to be that data—necessary for an answer that will satisfy mind and heart.

There are a number of steps. Believing in God does not mean surrender to absurdity. For believers at least, faith is the supremely meaningful act. The question that aches in all our efforts to know is: What does it all finally mean? We hunger for meaning and cannot live without it. It is our essential sustenance. In the search for meaning, human knowledge has expanded in a myriad ways— the knowledge explosion of our times. Our minds expand in a

---

* W. Norris Clarke, S. J., "Is Natural Theology still viable today?," in *Prospects for Natural Theology*, E. Long (ed.), Catholic University of America Press, Washington, 1992, p. 181.

world of meaning. We are plunged into a limitless, meaningful world that emerges more and more brightly as the human mind explores it. We are participating in a universe of meaning and existing in an intelligible world that cannot be explained by mere chance. Science and scholarship collaborate in celebrating the fact that questions do have answers and that reality is astonishingly meaningful.

To believe in the one God is to have a sense that there is a meaning, an ultimate all-comprehending meaning, implicit in all meaningful explorations: "In your light we see light" (Ps 36:9).

Just as believing in God is not an opting for absurdity but a celebration of meaning, neither is it a lack of concern for the truth. The believer is not committed to an untruth or a lie, nor evading, in some infantile way, the truth that hurts. The fact that the human mind can establish the truth of anything, the sufficient reason for anything, arises from a sense, however implicit, that there is a sufficient reason for everything. We believe in God as the final truth—the sufficient reason for all our sufficient reasons. Hence God is affirmed as the solid ground and foundation of truthful existence.

Thirdly, believing in God is not immoral, but an assent to the supreme good and value. We believe in God as the abiding worthwhileness of everything we most prize. The fact that our conscience can find its peace only in honesty, justice, and generosity intimates that we live in a universe in which our moral values are grounded in an original goodness and original love. Hence, believing in the one God is to affirm that moral decisions really count in a value-friendly universe.

Fourthly, believing in God is not a self-destructive option, a move away from who or what we are individually and together. Believing means living in the presence of that One for which our personal being most hungers for its affirmation and fulfillment. Our hearts home in on the supremely personal reality, on the One in whom we are most alive, in whose embrace each of us comes home, as named and recognised and destined for the fullness of life.

In other words, even before God is revealed in a special way, all human beings are involved in an elemental love-affair with the infinite (cf. Sebastian Moore). To exist as a human person is to be waiting on this One to manifest itself. Faith occurs when love answers to the Word spoken to a listening creation, and as the Spirit meets and expands our spiritual searching. Thus, faith recognizes that from the beginning we are standing on holy ground. The One was always there ... St Anselm in the first chapter of his *Prosologion* prays in words applicable to us all:

> Teach me to seek you and reveal yourself to me as I seek, because I can neither seek you if you do not teach me how, nor find you unless you reveal yourself. Let me seek you in desiring you; let me desire you in seeking you; let me find you in loving you; let me love you in finding you.*

* Quoted in *The Divine Office*, I, E. J. Dwyer, Sydney, 1974, p. 68.

6

THE FATHER

The one God is first of all invoked as "Father." The original source "who has blessed us in Christ with every spiritual blessing," who has chosen us in Christ "before the foundation of the world" to be present to him in love, is named and confessed as the "Father of our Lord Jesus Christ" (Eph 1:3–4). God is "Father" in relation to the Son, as the giver of the Son, and as "gather[ing] up all things in him, things in heaven and things on earth" (Eph 1:10).

The naming of God as Father is part of the fundamental movement of thanksgiving, of *eucharistia*: in faith, thanking precedes and accompanies all thinking. The one God is identified as Father, as the source of all that has come to us in Christ:

> May you be made strong with all the strength that
> comes from his glorious power, and may you be
> prepared to endure everything with patience, while
> joyfully giving thanks to the Father, who has enabled
> you to share in the inheritance of the saints in the light.
> He has rescued us from the power of darkness and
> transferred us into the kingdom of his beloved Son, in
> whom we have redemption, the forgiveness of sins.
> (Col 1:11–14)

Many of the themes of the creed are adumbrated in Paul's prayer. For the moment we shall emphasize the eucharistic recognition of God as the Father of the Son. Believers stand before God participating in the Son's relationship to the One from whom he comes, in whose presence he lives, and to whom he has returned. As sons and daughters in the Son, we are freed to be free with God. God is not called first of all master, as though we were slaves, or even king as though we were subjects, or even father in a generalized metaphorical sense as creator of the world, let alone as oppressive patriarch. The Christian invocation of God as Father lives from the memory of Jesus' intimate relationship with God, expressed in the familiar address, "Abba, Father!" God is named, then, as the Father in the human language of the Son. The Father is the One to whom Jesus is turned in the totality of his existence and as the One from whom he possesses his deepest identity and mission. Our intimate invocation of God as Father derives from Jesus' own style of relating to God (Mk 14:36, Mt 11:27 and parallels). The invocation of God as "Father" is essential to his prayer and central in the vocabulary of his self-expression.

The One from and for whom Jesus lived is now "Our Father." Our freedom with God is strikingly expressed by Paul:

> For you did not receive a spirit of slavery to fall back
> into fear, but you have received a spirit of adoption.
> When we cry, "Abba! Father!" it is that very Spirit
> bearing witness with our spirit that we are children of
> God. (Rom 8:15–16)

God is so invoked on the basis of Jesus' relationship to the source of life that has begotten him, and reveals itself in him: "No one comes to the Father except through me" (Jn 14:6). Any attempt to go to the Father outside the way of Jesus may say a lot about human projection and fear, or the ambiguous religiosity of the human condition, or even about the unknowable ways in which God is the living atmosphere of all lives. But through, with, and in Jesus, faith identifies God as the One who, in self-giving love, is revealed in the Son: "Whoever has seen me has seen the Father" (Jn 14:9).

The credal confession of God as "Father" is, then, not the glorification or idolization of parental power and authority. It flows from God's self-utterance in the Son. The Father gives what is most intimate to himself, "the beloved Son," into the darkness of human existence, "to the point of death—even death on a cross" (Phil 2:8). This original self-giving Love is revealed as unconditional, a love that keeps on being love even at the most intense point of the world's evil: the cross.

Further, the divine character of this original, self-giving, unconditional love has affirmed and acknowledged the Son by raising him in the glory of the resurrection.

Hence, far from being a general metaphor of God as parent, the Father is the name of One who is the source of all that Jesus is, in himself and "for us." The source of this "for us-ness" is the self-giving God, God as ecstatically open to the other, the Father begetting and communicating himself to the Son.

Hence, God is invoked as Father only as the fulfillment of our Christian experience of God. There is a certain danger in thinking of the Father as the first divine person—as though we know who the Father is apart from Christ and his Spirit. It is helpful to realize that in our experience of God, the Spirit tends to come first. For the Spirit of holiness inspires communion and intimacy with the one God and with all in God. Penetrated by that presence, faith may well awake to a nameless mystery of love and holiness, waiting for it to declare itself. It rests, but cannot be content: who is this other moving within the heart and expanding it with all kinds of intimations and hopes? Will such love ever declare itself and show its face and speak a word?

Faith flowers in human history when it picks up in Jesus the resonance of all its secret knowing and hopes. Christians find in him the utterance and declaration of what they have been living and looking for. As the Word incarnate, he is the form and embodiment of the gift intimately offered, but hardly named.

Faith unfolds in communication with Jesus, the Son. Through union with him, in eating and drinking the reality of all that Christ is, the believer is nourished into a new sense of God as the all-inclusive, gracious mystery. It is self-revealed in the Son and given in the Spirit. The Father's engendering love reaches into the depths of our being to expand what we are into pure God-wardness:

> And because you are children, God has sent the Spirit of his Son into our hearts, crying "Abba! Father!" So you are no longer a slave but a child, and if a child then also an heir, through God. (Gal 4:6–7)

Nourished by the Word and indwelt by the Spirit, we "dare to say, Our Father" (the *audemus dicere* of the old Latin liturgy)—to invoke God as the origin and end of all that moves within us as true life. The Father is the One in whose spacious house there are "many dwelling places" (Jn 14:2).

To ignore the interior role of the Spirit in the dynamic of becoming intimate with God is to risk misplacing the invocation of God as Father. The danger occurs in either of two ways. At one extreme we can simply idolize human authority, especially in its male cultural forms. As a result, genuine adoration of God the Father is compromised by reverence for a patriarchal idol. In such a context, Jesus appears as a kind of compensation for a distorted idea of God, while the neglected Spirit arrives as an optional consolation, once the real work of revelation has been accomplished. Or, at the opposite extreme, by rejecting all reverence for authority in the name of some spiritual freedom, we can easily fall into a kind of isolated self-absorption in which the basic symbols of faith are reduced to private narcissistic fantasy. The Spirit is no longer the Spirit of the crucified Jesus in a community of self-transcending love, and the Father is replaced by a "father image" manipulated as an escape from the real adult world.

In contrast to both these perversions, the creed's confession of the one God, the Father, takes us to the heart of the Gospel narrative. Here, believers find themselves included in the autobiography of God:

> I have made your name known to those whom you gave me from the world. They were yours, and you gave them to me, and they have kept your word. Now they know that everything you have given me is from you; for the words that you gave to me I have given to them, and

they have received them and know in truth that I came
from you. (Jn 17:6–8)

The One who expresses himself in his Word, in the beloved
Son, draws believers into the realm of new life: "And this is eternal
life, that they may know you, the only true God, and Jesus Christ
whom you have sent" (Jn 17:3). This divine love-life is charac-
terized by familiarity with the divine origin and with him who has
come forth as the only-begotten Son. God can be addressed as
Father because God has been revealed as original and sovereign
love, proving itself in the life, death, and resurrection of Jesus, and
in the outpouring of the Spirit.

While the Father dwells within those who love the Son (Jn
15:23), he is not "sent" in the way the Son and Spirit are given to
us. He comes to us as the abiding source of both the Son and the
Spirit, in the intimacy of personal, loving presence.

In its familiarity with the Father as the loving source of life,
faith experiences that perfect love that casts out fear (1 Jn 4:18).
To believe is to stand in the presence of God in thanksgiving, in
intimacy with the One who is self-given in the Son and the Spirit.

The rest of the creed unfolds for the believer the depth and
breadth of the Father's giving.

Despite the modern ambivalence in regard to any "father-
image" and the feminist criticism of the long history of patriarchy,
the Christian symbol of the Father holds within it a further depth
of meaning. It accents the transcendent, prodigal freedom of God.
Christian intimacy with the divine, the wholly Other, does not
happen in an automatic, quasi-natural fashion. Faith is not simply
a kind of symbiosis with the divine. We are drawn into communion
with God as receivers of a gift. Though we are summoned into
existence and its freedom, our intimacy with the divine is beyond
any ambit of natural evolution. God is not simply the womb of
nature. Divine love acts in unconditioned freedom to bring forth
our own free self-surrender to the way of the Crucified.

The authentic Christian meaning of the Fatherhood of God
does not excuse the extreme masculinism of much religious
language. The sediment of past epochs of patriarchal experience
lies thick on our present powers of expression. It tends to make us

forget the subversive intimacy of Jesus' invocation of God as Father and the provocation inherent in his prohibition "call no one your father" (Mt 23:9) in the undifferentiated patriarchal culture of his day.

The present situation invites exploration in two ways. The first lies in appreciating the original context of the Christian invocation of God as "Abba, Father," as we outlined above. Secondly, while the name, "Father," is proper to the first divine person, the metaphor of divine fatherhood must live in a larger frame of gracious reference. It has to be set in the larger context of other symbols—feminine, maternal, spousal, even inanimate (for example, the ocean, the heights, light, fire, wind ...). The language of poets and mystics and philosophers, the studies of psychologists, educators and theologians, converge on the task of taking us back to the freshness and liberation of Jesus' original invocation of God as Father. If this ceases to be an invocation of God that is subversive of cultural idols, if it no longer seems to provoke an intimate and gracious sense of relationship to the all-inclusive mystery, something is deeply disturbed in Christian communication.

No doubt any culture tends to domesticate the divine in a mono-dimensional fantasy apt to nourish the prevailing ideology. No particular divine name can be so absolute as to curtail the whole play of language in its celebration of the infinities of God's life and love. In no social or cultural context is reference to God a matter of simple semantics or dead metaphors. If faith is to remain alive to the living God, if it is to serve the Word, and communicate in the Spirit, our language needs to be restlessly imaginative.

For instance, the Gospel narrative of how God is revealed as Father raises the question of how Mary is a living icon of the divine, as Mother of God, *Theotokos*. This is a somewhat neglected question in current theology and spirituality. It can be posed in these words: How does the motherhood of Mary affect our sense of the Fatherhood of God? In the long history of Catholic and Orthodox liturgical and spiritual traditions, the answer is found only on a lived, implicit level. In the current ecumenical re-appraisal of the place of Mary in scripture and tradition, a richer theology promises to develop.

Even more fundamentally, we may follow the lead given in the fourth chapter of John's first letter, in which God is described as "Love." This can lead to an appreciation of how the reality of God is a "love-life," and of how an infinite divine consciousness of "being in love" is the matrix in which the holy Trinity emerges. The mystery of love is, then, the divine womb of relational and self-giving life in which the Father is known and named: "everyone who loves is born of God and knows God. Whoever does not love does not know God, for God is love" (1 Jn 4:7–8).

These two instances do not seem irrelevant to our current problems in regard to inclusive language.

7

THE ALMIGHTY

Just as the creed corrects our idolization of God as a patriarchal power, so, too, it subverts any notion we have of the divine omnipotence as limitless caprice. God's "glorious power" (Col 1:11) is defined in terms of the reality of Christ and the Spirit, and as relative to the free creation the Father is calling into being.

The almighty character of God (*omnipotens*; *pantokrator*) means that there is nothing outside God's creative and providential scope. The whole of history unfolds before the Father's gaze, to be brought to its climax in the life, death, and resurrection of Jesus, the only Son. Confessing "The Almighty" in these terms makes the creed an expression of limitless hope:

> Now to him who by the power at work within us is able
> to accomplish abundantly far more than all we can ask
> or imagine, to him be glory in the church and in Christ
> Jesus to all generations, forever and ever. Amen.
> (Eph 3:20–21)

Hence, divine omnipotence is not an unbridled force meant to stun and shock creation with some kind of super-energy. The power of God works, as Elijah experienced it, "as the sound of sheer silence." In the creed's emphasis, the Father is the almighty God as the source of the "impossible" works of love. God's power works to give creation the surprise of God's own involvement with our humanity, beyond the scope of what eye can see and ear hear or the human heart conceive. Inherent in God's life-giving power is a divine vulnerability. God refuses to appear in our world save in the form of the crucified humanity of the Son. In this sense, the crucified Christ is both "the power of God and the wisdom of God" (1 Cor 1:24).

As a result, the almighty character of God as Father is primarily instanced in the unreserved, supremely personal gift. Only God can communicate in this way. In our world of finite persons, we enter relationships, make gestures, and put ourselves into works of love in various ways, perhaps to a degree of great generosity. In the end, however, we have to acknowledge a limit beyond which our kind of loving is either self-destructive for ourselves or oppressive of the other—or, more likely, both. For instance, if you try to give yourself totally to those you love without accepting your limits in terms of time, energy, and personal capacity, you end up giving to others only a tired, exhausted shell of yourself. Such an outcome is somewhat less than the gift was intended to be! As for the receiver of such love, if any of us tries to enter into the very being of the other, to become his or her total life, a destructive possessiveness and limitation of the true being of the other is the sad result. In contrast, as the one mystery utters itself in the Word and communicates itself in the Spirit, God alone is inexhaustibly complete and life-giving in love. As the Word becomes flesh with us (God-with-us), the Spirit (God-within-us) enables our acceptance of the Word in our hearts. The omnipotence of God's love is revealed in the unreserved character of its giving. It is not lessened by what it gives, nor does it diminish those who receive it. It is almighty in Word and in Spirit. The gift of God is sheer grace.

Further, divine love is almighty in the way it both respects and enhances human freedom. Divine freedom does not compete with human freedom, but creates, enlarges, and fulfills our liberty. The omnipotence of love can pluck out the heart of stone and replace it with the heart of flesh (Ezek 36:26). Where the human autocrat exercises power over others, the Almighty works within the freedom of the human heart. God is present to the depths of our freedom as our creator and fulfillment. Through God's action,

Saul of Tarsus becomes Paul the apostle. The greater our freedom, the more creative our response, the more the omnipotent freedom of God is glorified.

God's power manifests itself in patience. God has time for the whole of human history to grow to its own grandeur and scope. Nor are the almighty ways of love defeated by human evil. The transforming power of God is incalculably at work. Though it is patient, it is not endlessly frustrated or held in reserve. In the resurrection of Jesus, the power of love is already manifest in an irreversible manner. Love has come to its own victory, but in a way proportioned to God's allowance for the whole history of faith. The true power of God is offered to us, not as a brute force, but in the inexhaustible imagination of love.

For love to be omnipotent means that it is not constrained by human conditions, even those resulting from human guilt and incapacity:

> And by this we will know that we are from the truth
> and will reassure our hearts before him whenever our
> hearts condemn us; for God is greater than our hearts,
> and he knows everything. (1 Jn 3:19–20)

The incarnational focus of God's action neither destroys nor metabolizes our humanity into something else. Loved in our human reality, we are not transmogrified into some kind of super-humanity. Nonetheless, God is present to the human in love's transforming power. In this regard the key parable of transformation is the paschal mystery of Jesus Christ: though the Word becomes flesh, right down to the limits of death and burial among the dead, he is raised up as "the resurrection and the life"(cf. Jn 11:25).

God is the power of life beyond the limits of any self-making of our own. There is a realm of life we can enter only by receiving it, only as a gift, only as grace: "All things can be done for the one who believes" (Mk 9:23). What for us is impossible, even as we long for the eternities of life and love and universal communion, is not so for almighty love at work through the universe: "For mortals it is impossible, but not for God; for God all things are possible" (Mk 10:27).

Human beings, then, are not agents of their own transformation. We must wait on the gift, yield to the transforming energy of the Spirit, and receive the vitalizing power of the vine of which we are branches: "apart from me you can do nothing" (Jn 15:5). To be human is to exist at God's mercy.

The credal confession of God's almighty love is, then, the foundation of hope. It precludes any totalizing of the human predicament in terms of suffering, guilt, moral impotence, death, and failure. An always greater power is at work to counter the apathy nourishing itself on the despairing judgment that "it is all over"—with ourselves, with others, or with the world itself. In that hopelessness, death has the last word and the sum of the world's possibilities is fixed in the way things are. But working within, with, and through that totality of the way things are is the limitless power of love.

The recognition of our human limits does not leave us there. At that brink of existence, the impossible possibilities of what only God can do are present.

By the same token, belief in the almighty, all-comprehending compass of God's power and presence is not to be edged out in favor of some form of evolutionary optimism—as though the automatic unfolding of nature and the cosmos was itself the ultimate power in the universe. An evolutionary or processive understanding of the world can be entirely appropriate in scientific terms. On the other hand, the almighty love of God is not compromised by the all-encompassing power of the cosmic process or biological evolution—if only for the reason that the cosmic unfolding or biological evolution or historical progress leaves behind a trail of tragedy and death. What happens is such a strange mixture of order and chance that the human mind is left ever vacillating between the two. For, to the judgment of science, the cosmic process unfolds indifferent to individual fate or even the continuance of the species—perhaps even to the perdurance of life itself.

In contrast, the almighty power that is the object of faith and the ground of hope is intensely personal. In the eternity of love, no one is left behind, no one generation is closer to God than another. Those who have died out of the world, those who have given their lives for the sake of others, are not mere raw material for progress. They have died into the depths of love's mystery at work, and are contained in its presence. God forgets no one, least of all those buried in a mass grave.

The omnipotence of love is not a "theory of everything," as contemporary science might envisage it. For the "Father, the Almighty" is affirmed only through adoration, and in surrender to the infinite self-giving love that leaves nothing and no one outside its purpose. In the confession of such a hope, what we most love is not left to the mercy of what we most fear, but offered into the impossible possibilities of God: "But if God so clothes the grass of the field, which is alive today and tomorrow is thrown into the oven, how much more will he clothe you—you of little faith!" (Lk 12:28). Our "little faith" must be open to the extent of what God can do, and is doing, through the whole of creation, "for us ... and our salvation."

Admittedly, the totality of what is in the making cannot be known to us. It must be left to the infinity of love that operates in God's way and in God's time. Still, the basic icon of the emerging wholeness of creation is the risen Christ. The power to transform and raise up is extended through him to the whole of creation and history. Nothing and no one is outside its universal care: "We know that all things work together for good for those who love God, who are called according to his purpose" (Rom 8:28).

Here the agony of Jesus exemplifies that great groaning totality of the universe awaiting the transformation that only the ultimate Source of life can give, in God's way and in God's good time: "Abba, Father, for you all things are possible; remove this cup from me ... " (Mk 14:36).

To confess God as "Almighty" is to have the assurance that Love will be revealed for what it is. Divine creativity is not diminished by working in and through the human. Nor is it checked by the power of evil, as though evil were the ultimate determinant of the universe. Nor is the love of God changed into vengeance by the machinations of human evil, even when human sin crucifies the redeemer himself. The divine power of love will not be compromised by descending to the level of the world's power-play. Just as Jesus, the Son, rejects the way of violence and worldly ambition in obedience to the Father, the character of the Father is revealed in his refusal to act in any way other than that of the crucified humanity of the Son: "This is my Son, the Beloved; listen to him!" (Mk 9:7). In such exchanges, the Spirit too is revealed, not as a demonic power, but as the field of love inviting all who believe into the self-giving life of both the Father and the Son.

In the face of evil, love radiates in a new intensity. The divine capacity to turn evil into good displays itself as mercy and forgiveness. The unspent resources of love break the vicious circle of revenge and domination. To adore such omnipotence demands the moral risk of being "merciful, just as your Father is merciful" (Lk 6:36). Christian faith moves in a world where a limitless love, seemingly defenseless in the real world, is the ultimately victorious power:

> If God is for us, who is against us? He who did not
> withhold his own Son, but gave him up for all of us,
> will he not with him also give us everything else? ... No,
> in all these things we are more than conquerors through
> him who loved us. For I am convinced that neither
> death, nor life, nor angels, nor rulers, nor things
> present, nor things to come, nor powers, nor height, nor
> depth, nor anything else in all creation, will be able to
> separate us from the love of God in Christ Jesus our
> Lord. (Rom 8:31–39)

God's love, then, manifests its power in opposition to the omnipotent pretensions of human culture—"the rulers and powers" of this world. It is subversive of the pretensions to omnipotence that are the root of individual or global self-destruction. In the guise of a humble and vulnerable love, the Almighty occupies the last place in this world. There it works to exorcise our most familiar demon, the lust for power that infests human history. It alone can topple the idols that obscure our true finiteness and mask our dependence on the truly infinite. The Father, the Almighty, acting in the subversive force of love, leaves us with nothing but the disarmed reality of our own humanity—yet as loved by God and offered true life as a gift: "God's foolishness is wiser than human wisdom, and God's weakness is stronger than human strength" (1 Cor 1:25).

All prayer finds a secure foundation in the creed's sense of the almighty character of God. By surrendering to God's all-pervading action in the world, believers dwell in the unfinished chaos of the world in prayer and intercession. As the whole of creation groans in the great act of bringing forth the fullness of Christ's humanity, in hope, longing, and petition we groan within it. Within that tension toward the fullness of things, the Spirit groans within us, enlarging the span of our hopes and making our prayers responsive to the ultimate designs of the Lord (Rom 8:22–25). Prayer—asking, seeking, knocking at the door—is our distinctive participation in God's almighty love. Praying within the limits of our time and place, we are doing what God is doing in the universe.

The seeming powerlessness of prayer involves us in the most life-giving and ultimate of all energies. For it is not as though God is changed by our prayers, as though our Father is insensitive to some detail of possible good. Rather, the sheer bounty of God's love changes believers into intercessors to open their lives and their world to the ultimate gift.

In the experience of prayer we become familiar with the manner in which God's almighty power works in our world. God does not act as one more vector of forces among countless others. Rather God works in all causes, acts in all activities, not from the outside but from within the reality and dynamics of the world of divine creation. As Creator and Redeemer, God is intimately self-involved: climactically in the incarnation and the indwelling Spirit, but also in all the push and the pulls that determine our lives, in all the influences from above and from below, in the formation of the structures that determine our being, in the information that guides them, and in the transformation that awaits them. Everything issues from the Almighty, but with the gentleness of light, and in both the patience and the impatience of love.

When all is said and done, God is almighty, not in the sense of being capriciously at work from beyond our world, but as integrating all that makes up our world into the love's ultimate and all-inclusive purpose—to communicate the divine self to creation.

In summing up, the words of the ancient sage of Israel cannot be bettered:

> We could say more but could never say enough; let the
> final word be: "He is the all."... For he is greater than
> all his works ... Glorify the Lord and exalt him as much
> as you can, for he surpasses even that ... do not grow
> weary, for you cannot praise him enough. (Sir 43:27–30)

8

The Maker of Heaven and Earth

maker of heaven and earth,
of all that is, seen and unseen.

MAKER

The distinctive way in which "the Father, the Almighty" is the primordial maker of everything is usually expressed in the term "Creator." The divine mode of making and doing and acting is creating. God's creative activity is expressed in a great variety of images in the scriptures Christians share with Israel (cf. Gen 1–3; Sir 16:26–17:19; Wis 7:22–25).

God's making extends to all that is—in all the tenses of the verb "to be" and all the modes of actual and possible being—all that is, was, and will be; in all its being and becoming; everything that I am, you are, we are, they are, it is; in all the differences and relationships and creativity implied in *all* of this. If this is so, God's way of making is not like any other kind of action or creativity contained within the bounds of "heaven and earth."

God is uniquely the Creator. The almighty Father is not busy in the great process of the universe as a particular agent alongside the rest of known, or as yet unknown, agents and energies that make things the way they are. God's making is different. The divine agent is present at the roots of all existence and in all the creatures' capacity to act. The creative activity of God is not set simply alongside the rest, as one factor, however important, in the varied influences that determine the shape of the real. For God acts out of sheer originality. As the source of all being, the Creator God is the ground of why there is something rather than nothing, the inclusive cause of all being and becoming. This gives rise to a number of wonderful insights that are the common possession of our religious tradition.

In the first place, as Creator, the one God is more intimately present to creation than the creature is to itself. God's act is revealed in both our being and our becoming. The more the creature comes to be, the higher the degree of our life and love and creativity, the more God is involved and expressed, and the more, indeed, do we participate in the creativity of the divine. Our capacity as persons to be and to act is the outcome of what God has done, and is doing, in creating what and who we are in the wonder of existence. The divine Being is the limitless matrix in whom "we live and move and have our being" (Acts 17:28), present in all that is as "one God and Father of all, who is above all and through all and in all" (Eph 4:6).

Secondly, in creating the universe, God acts freely. What is created is neither necessary nor an automatic overflow from some great reservoir of being. God's creative freedom is unconditioned; it depends on nothing external to itself. The acknowledgment of God's freedom in creating is the first step in realising that creation is loved into being. At the source of all creation is the exuberance of infinite love: the universe, and everyone and everything in it, is primarily a gift. Since creation need not have happened, the universe of all that is, in its very fabric and every fiber, is given into existence, loved into being, and occurs as a gift.

Thirdly, the divine creative act presupposes nothing. As sheer gift, the universe is made "out of nothing." God has acted so that something other than God should exist to share in divine joy, to receive the gift and the giving that God is, for the sake of that perfect fulfillment when "God will be all in all" (1 Cor 15:28). Though we cannot but imagine some kind of raw material or a prior universal process conditioning the way God creates, the mind comes to a point of wonder in understanding that any such material or any such process is itself created. The divine freedom presupposes nothing except the divine creativity itself.

More deeply still, there is no goodness prior to God's action or apart from the goodness of God itself that might somehow attract the Creator into the act of creating. For the only goodness prior to creation is God's own: "the love of God infuses and creates the goodness in reality" (*amor Dei infundens et creans bonitatem in rebus*) as St Thomas Aquinas notes (*Summa Theologica*, I, q. 20, a. 2). The universe as a whole and in each of its particulars, in all its structures and processes, is loved into being. The Infinite Good spreads itself, shares itself, gives itself in order that all other goodness might exist and be enjoyed.

Fourthly, if creation is not like any other kind of making or doing, how can we speak of it within our world of limited making and doing? Our language must be analogical (as explained in chapter 2). We can dimly describe the divine creative act only in terms of our human experience of making and producing. Take the example of artistic creativity. In a moment of inspiration, the artist is possessed of profound, original creativity. That moment of inspiration animates all the distinct actions and elements involved in the production of any work of art. All the varied elements and phases, be they notes or words or paint strokes or shapes or movements, are born out of an imaginative conception of the whole. The creative moment, as distinct from the demanding effort to "realize" it, to give it concrete form in a certain medium, is experienced as wonderfully "given." As it springs forth in the fertility of the artistic imagination, it already contains the whole of what is to be produced or performed. Of course, the transforming moment of real art is prepared for by the long formation of the artist in a chosen medium. Even Mozart had to practice his scales, learn from others, and become familiar with the capacities and limitations of the various instruments at his disposal. But within those limits, his originality was seemingly limitless; and the world continues to enjoy his amazing art. Along with all artists in their respective media, he gave expression to what was original within him in what was other than him—the notes, the scales, the harmonies, and the instruments he employed. The ecstatic self-expression of all artists so affects our lives that our shared human world is lifted out of its routine shapes or sound or color or form and movement to a point of surprise, excess, and wonder. It can never be the same again.

Artistic creativity can be taken as a dim metaphor for divine creation. God's creative action wells up, as it were, from the divine imagination, as utter originality. For in the divine act of creation, no prior medium is presupposed, nor is there any other to appreciate it—except insofar as it too is created. God is pure originality, pure self-expression. It brings forth what is other than God not only so that this other—these others, for we are included!—is the expression of the divine goodness and beauty, but also so that this other might share, in its own scope for self-expression, in the creative love of God.

Though the word "incarnation" is usually reserved for the Word made flesh in Jesus Christ, we can understand creation in a more general sense as an incarnation of the love and imagination of God. This cosmic incarnation finds its culminating moment in the personal self-expression that occurs when the Word personally becomes flesh. In Jesus Christ, the original meaning and promise of creation takes explicit shape.

Then, there is another analogical way of understanding what creation means. The original human community is made in God's self-image: "'Let us make humankind in our image, according to our likeness' ... male and female he created them" (Gen 1:26–27). Living images of their Creator, human beings, in the generative capacities of body and spirit, go on to "make" one another in love and communication. Through the creativity of nature and culture, we love one another into being in a way that far transcends any ordinary instrumental meaning of "making." We can make someone, not merely something. This communal, mutual creativity, through all the exchanges of human relationships, actively shares in the divine creativity imaged in our coexistence. In this experience of "making" one another, we grow to a deeper sense of how God makes us and the universe in which we exist.

Fifthly, we are finally led to the most intimate understanding of creation as it is envisaged in the creed. All divine making flows from the trinitarian life of God. In that primordial mystery, divine reality unfolds in an original self-expression, the Word and Son, and in an ecstatic self-giving as the Spirit is breathed forth. Creation is an extension into time of these eternal processions. As a divine self-expression and as a divine gift, it bears traces (*vestigia*) of its trinitarian origin: in the sheer wonder of existing, as coming forth from nothing, creation radiates a sense of the limitless being of the One who is, the eternal origin, Father. In its particularity and varied forms, as *this* rather than *that*, in *this* kind of universe, the created universe participates in the divine self-expression characteristic of the Word. The creation, as an interconnected and interrelated whole tending in the direction of greater communion and deeper life, images forth the presence of the Spirit. Creation in its deepest reality is an icon of the Trinity.

The iconic trinitarian form of creation crystalizes in its final beauty when, through the power of the Spirit, the Word becomes flesh. Once again we glimpse how the perfect form and deepest meaning of creation is uniquely embodied in Jesus Christ: "He is the image of the invisible God, the firstborn of all creation" (Col 1:16).

OF HEAVEN AND EARTH

The all-inclusive character of God's creation is expressed in the phrase "maker of heaven and earth." That is to say that there is nothing outside the scope of divine creativity. Here God holds together what we characteristically keep apart as two separate domains, the heavenly and the earthly. There are a number of implications.

First, the scope of God's creative activity and presence is not limited to a purely spiritual creation, as though the divine were involved exclusively with the soul and with spiritual realities only. God also creates matter and all the physical energies presupposed in the structure and processes of the world as it is—the inanimate, the biological, and all the pre-personal structures, forms, and dynamics that, one way or another, support our human existence. We might also add the sexual which, to say the least, has been rather unevenly accommodated in our spiritual traditions.

Today it is important to underscore the involvement of God in material creation for two reasons. First, because modern scientific exploration of the physical origins of the universe is in awe at the quite uncanny emergence and astonishingly inter-connected totality of the physical world. This cannot be dismissed as of no religious value. Admittedly, religion has been tradition-ally more at home with spiritual realities, with "heaven" and with "the unseen." For its part, modern scientific culture has become marvelously familiar with "earth," "the seen," and the material. Despite the tension resulting from such different emphases, Christian belief in creation insists that the two are related in the one reality of God's creative self-expression.

And there is a second reason. Stalking religious consciousness down the ages has been a sense of some other kind of creation—a material, limiting, or even evil principle somehow coexistent with, and even resistant to, God's creative power—a kind of shadow-side of reality. Such dualism tended to make the religious mind intolerant of the bodily and the material. It gave a bias toward a spirituality nourished exclusively on the invisible, as if we human beings were pure spirits haunting the earth instead of inhabiting it. Such spirituality tended to mean an escape from the physical by consigning matter to the realm of inferior or spurious reality.

In Christian history, the Manichaean heresy was the most virulent expression of the tendency to dematerialize the whole goodness of creation. Preceding such a position, however benignly, was an anti-matter, anti-body influence stemming from classical Platonism. As a result, down the ages mutilated versions of Christianity have been both deeply suspicious of the body and sexuality, and hostile toward scientific activity because of its involvement with physical reality.

In contrast, the movement of God's creation is toward incarnation: the invisible embodied in the visible; the divine mystery present in the physical and material. God's creative love encompasses both heaven and earth, to bring the two together in the one blessed creation. The polarities present in our one human existence are not competing dualisms. There is no rivalry between these two dimensions of created existence. Genuine spirituality does not demean the respective roles of the material and the physical, of the bodily and the sexual, or of the scientific exploration of matter. Nor does true worldliness, basing itself on a connection with the earth and concern for its future, mean a lessening of contact with the transcendent, the divine, the spiritual, the heavenly.

Because both polarities in our experience, the spiritual and the material, belong to the one divine creation, the creed insists on their interrelationship. We ignore either at our peril, and unite both for our ultimate well-being. A holistic sense of creation demands that faith makes room for the proper independence of the secular, the true value of the world in itself. Our hope for the life of the world to come cannot demean the worth of our present life in this world. For its part, the secular will mutilate its full meaning if it represses the domain of the spiritual. Cut off from ultimate hope, it will be going nowhere: God is the maker of heaven *and* earth.

A second general point is this. A sense of the one-ness of God's creation demands that believers bear the whole grace and the whole weight of that creation. As complex beings, we praise the creator in and through that complexity. Whatever the diversity in our callings and life-styles, and the philosophies that justify them, the creed excludes any monodimensional vision of existence. It likewise stands against any dualism that so compartmentalizes our experience that no underlying unity in the one creation can be acknowledged. To that degree, belief in God as maker of heaven and earth keeps us in a salutary state of complexity. If we are to live in the simplicity of adoring God as Creator, we have to make room for the complexity of everything.

Accepting all reality as God's creation leads to a sense of "the all" and "the whole" as a *universe*. This is at once to respect and to go beyond the way modern science conceives of the physical cosmos. While faith need have no problems with the brilliance of modern grand unified theories, or with some final "theory of everything," it must insist that such theories remain open to the transcendent origin, form, and goal of the totality of material and spiritual existence. Only as created by God is reality in all its aspects, phases, levels, structures, and dimensions finally appreciated as a "uni-verse," the one reality of creation. Belief in the Creator supports the most comprehensively holistic appreciation of reality: it puts the "-holic" in the *catholic*, the universal dimension of Christian faith. We can go further still, for God is "the maker ..."

OF ALL THAT IS

Belief in creation attunes faith to recognize the universe as a great symphonic event. Nothing in all its manifold dimensions of order and spontaneity, of nature and history, is outside the scope of God's creative activity. God's making includes the past, present, and future; and all the dynamics of cosmic emergence, biological evolution, spiritual freedom, intellectual achievement, artistic expression, and ethical action. God creates not merely "things," but all the variety and levels of conscious existence, in which the great symphony of creation springs into awareness. Since God is the source of all that is, everything and everyone is interrelated in the one universe of creation. Each element and event participates in its own particular way in the one universal event of what God has made, and is making.

The universe is the totality of what is, of all that is already known or is yet to be discovered. The "We/I believe" of the creed occurs within the *It* of the universe that has brought us forth, in the many billion years of cosmic history. The creed is sung on the air of one of the planets of one of the hundred billion stars of one of the hundred billion galaxies of the known cosmos. No doubt there are forces and energies, dimensions and life-forms that remain to be discovered (or rediscovered?). Note, here, the excess of reality that faith celebrates in its exuberant listing of ranks and hosts of angels. In adoring the Creator and in wonder at the expanse of the universe, the mind of faith is slow to believe that it is the only spiritual presence in the whole of God's creation. But wherever we turn, from quarks to quasars, from protons to supernovas, from the Big Bang to black holes, from the human brain to dark matter, from the beginnings of life to the defiant death of the martyr, from the brilliance of scientific exploration to the grandeur of simple moral goodness, from the human soul to the seraphim and archangels, there is one source from which everything derives.

Creation continues. God's creativity is not limited to the past. Unless the Creator continues to create, the universe will fall back into nothingness. Today, however, the continuing creative activity of God can be understood in greater depth. God's continuing creation not only prevents the universe from falling back into nothing, it enables it to increase its being in progressive levels of becoming. God creates the world not as a fundamentally finished reality, but as an expanding event. An all-engendering love is still at work, creating the universe in its capacity to become more, and to unfold to its ultimate dimensions. We can picture God creating the world less from "on high" and more as the infinite energy acting "from within," enabling existence to emerge into new intensities of communion and consciousness. As the Spirit of God acts within all the being and becoming, in all matter and life, it brings forth human consciousness. In the human mind and heart, the world becomes conscious of itself as a marvel of divine creation. In believers and contemplatives, creation becomes intimate with its source, to wait on the self-revelation of the reality from which everything has come forth.

In its coming forth from God, created reality is genuinely other than God. It is given to exist in its own real, finite right. It has its own freedom, spontaneity, and principles of action and interrelationship. The Creator God lets creation be itself. Being created does not mean that God crowds reality with a kind of overwhelming presence that never allows the creature to be genuinely other than God. Rather, created existence is a kind of dependent independence—dependent since God is always the ultimate ground of its being; independent since it truly does exist, with its own nature and scope of operation.

When thinking of God's creation as an act, we think of the total dependence everything has on God. When we consider *creation* as a noun, as the name of what God in fact has made and is making, we are struck more by the total independence it enjoys, right to the point, in the case of freedom, of standing for or against God. The Creator has risked, as it were, the true freedom of the creature. While this is an insoluble enigma, both sides of the reality of creation must be affirmed if we are to appreciate its mystery.

In creating, God is committed to having time for creation to be itself; to making space for what has come from the divine hand. It follows that God is not a big reality mixed in with the multiplicity of creation. For in its own domain, the world of creation is intelligible in its own right and on its own terms. Herein lies the foundation for the integrity of all scientific exploration. God does not distract from what God has made.

More practically, cosmology, physics, chemistry, biology, and psychology have their own subject matters. They are not to be confused with theology even if, as aspects of the one creation and as activities of the one created consciousness, all human modes of exploration properly exist in a dialogical relationship.

How confusion is to be prevented, how dialogue is to be carried out from the different perspectives on the one great fact of the existence of the universe, are exciting modern problems. The theology of creation reminds science that, in exploring any kind of reality, it is not edging out the reality of God. God is not part of creation, but the Creator acting both within and from beyond the scientifically accessible structures and dynamisms of all finite reality.

On the other hand, in exploring the reality of God we have no need to diminish or ignore any aspect of reality scientifically accessible to human investigation. For creation means that all is genuinely given to exist in its own right and with its own self-organizing powers.

And finally, the doctrine of creation, of how all beings are given into existence out of the generosity of Infinite Being, means that God is never foreign to creation. Everything is essentially related to God as its abiding source, sustenance, and goal. In the limited and varied being of the created universe, the sheer unlimited Being of God is, so to speak, materialized, embodied, expressed. The incarnation of the Word is, in the sense we suggested above, a culminating incarnation of God—the Word coming into his own, into what already is his, as the full, personal self-communication of God (Jn 1:11).

Belief in creation invites our minds to be untrammeled in the dynamism of exploration. When intelligence delights in what it achieved through the scientific explanation of the universe on intra-worldly terms, it is appreciating the genuine creative reality of mind in the midst of creation. But the mind can keep expanding as the reality it explores brims with questions: What is the explanation of all the explanations? What is the meaning of all the meaning we find? What is the reason for all the sufficient reasons we establish? Wherein lies the ultimate value of everything we have found worthwhile? Before whom do we finally stand, as we come to ourselves as unique persons, in the thinking, exploring, acting, creating, caring, and wondering of our lives?

In this way, belief in creation inspires the ultimate adventure in thinking, as the mind and heart refuse to rest in anything but the ultimately intelligible, the finally good, and the unified whole.

The creed's "all that is" includes the astonishing variety of real things, in all their interrelationships, processes, and levels of existence. Why is this "all" so intricately varied and differentiated? Evolutionary biology gives its answer in terms of the history of life's emergence. Physics and chemistry point to all the elements and forces and patterns necessary for the universe to be what it is. Modern ecological awareness appreciates the wondrous diversity and interconnectedness of life to warn us against limiting or upsetting it in any careless way. In pondering the question of why there is such variety in creation, St Thomas Aquinas gives a deceptively simple answer. God chose a varied creation to express more fully the richness of the divine being itself:

> God is ... the most perfect agent. Therefore, it belongs to
> him to induce his image in created things perfectly in the
> manner that befits created nature. But created things
> cannot attain to the perfect image of God in a single form:
> the cause exceeds the effect; for what exists in the cause in
> utter simplicity, is realized in the effect in a composite and
> pluriform manner ... It is fitting, then, that there be a
> multiplicity and variety in created things so that God's
> image be found in them perfectly in accord with their mode
> of being. (*Summa Contra Gentiles*, book 2, chapter 45)

But what of evil? That terrible question also lurks in "all that is." Disease, catastrophe, the perversions of human freedom, and death itself, permeate what God has created. If belief in creation excludes any evil principle in rivalry with God, why then is evil such a force, such a presence? Why is creation burdened with such a problem as evil? The history of Christian thinking largely leads to silence and waiting. We human beings would have more chance of hearing silence and seeing darkness than of understanding evil. It is the oppressive absence of the good we need and seek. The creed does not attempt any philosophical answer. It offers no solution except that of opening the way to a more complete surrender to the mystery of love, and of participating in its transforming and healing power. For the almighty source of love is likewise an excess beyond human comprehension. The excess of love is displayed as it exposes itself to our problem of evil in the incarnation, suffering, and death of the Son. It has already triumphed over evil in the resurrection of the Crucified. Such love shows its patience in having time for the whole of human history against the day of a final universal judgment when all evil will be revealed for what it is. In the meantime, the omnipotence of love assures us of the forgiveness of sins, and promises an ultimate transformation in "the life of the world to come."

There is, then, no instant solution for the conflicts and clashes, the destruction and limitations, the disease and ambiguity we experience. But in creating, the one God, the Father, the Almighty, promises an ultimate judgment, a universal moment of truth, to justify the divine way of creating and redeeming, and of allowing time and history to follow their course.

As faith waits for this final evidence, it is summoned to stand with the Son, who, "for us ... and our salvation," has immersed himself in the cosmic process and made himself vulnerable to the risk and tragedy of human history. A suffering creation finds its hope in the knowledge that God suffers our sufferings even more than we do ourselves.

The Song of the Three Jews calls us back from cosmic sadness to the defiant affirmation of universal praise. The inspired writer summons all the "works of the Lord" to "bless the Lord" (Dan 3:57). In our present knowledge of the wonder of the universe and emergence of life within it, such praise can be extended into a thousand other forms. The biblical prayer of praise runs through the realities of the natural world—sun and moon and stars, night and day, heat and cold, sea and dry land, wind and rain, animals, birds and fish, angels and human beings. But today the contemplative appreciation of the universe leaps to new possibilities. God can be glorified in the uncanny providence that guided the universe through its amazingly improbable journey to the present. At this moment, it brings us forth to an awareness of the vast, intricate scope of the universal event.

"Bless the Lord, all you works of the Lord!"—cosmic forces, galaxies in their billions, matter in all its varied forms, consciousness in all its glimmerings, both the sturdy predictabilities and the strange spontaneities of nature, its order and its chaos, in all the ten million species of living things with whom we share this planet, in every instant of the billions of years that have gone into our making, in all the elements of the stardust from which we are made: "to him be highest glory and praise forever."

SEEN AND UNSEEN

The radical wonder of creation does not limit either our faith or our knowledge to the invisible, to what is outside the immediate realm of human experience. It includes the visible. Faith's knowledge of God incorporates all reality. Prayer, contemplation, intelligence itself cannot exist save as earthed in what we see and taste, touch and smell, hear and feel. Sense, feeling, and imagination all delight in this world to bring home to the human mind and heart the mystery pervading all creation. Every level of our human awareness is united in faith's experience of the one creation in which everything is related.

This sense of universal interconnection is the foundation of all our analogical knowledge of God. The *invisible* is known through the *visible*. What is immediately accessible as, say, food and drink, as light and fire, as water and earth, as sexual love and family intimacy, is, in its largest frame of reference, a symbol of the beyond, of what is present but inexpressible. Above all, the humanity of Jesus is the incarnation of the divine. The Word made flesh is the ultimate analogy: "In him we see our God made visible, and so are caught up in love of the God we cannot see"

(The First Preface of Christmas). Flowing from the climactic event of the incarnation is the special sacramental awareness of faith. Familiar human symbols become "visible signs of invisible grace." More demandingly, our neighbor "whom [we] have seen," must be loved as condition of loving God "whom [we] have not seen" (1 Jn 4:20).

The creed, far from permitting a disjunction in our experience, unites the visible and invisible domains of reality as the one self-expression of God in creation. The visible is a path to the invisible, not a distraction from it. The invisible is incarnate in the visible, not concealed behind it. As St Augustine preached, "Through the invisible made visible, we pass from visible things to the invisible" (Christmas Day Sermon, c. 410 CE, *Sermo* 190.2).

Such a sense of creation provokes a distinctive kind of Christian realism. When ultimate reality is disclosed in the earthly, familiar realities of our immediate experience, the world cannot be treated as a mirage. It is not a veil behind which an unknowable and unknown reality is concealed. In the native patterns of human experience, reality is accessible, to be known and revealed in its ultimate dimensions.

The created totality in which the visible and invisible are related is the condition for the development of Christian civilization. The world of the senses, the expanding horizon of human meaning and value, the reality of the spiritual—all these are united in the one universe of God's creation. The instinct of Christian faith to embody itself in a given culture is, at root, a refusal to let the visible, the native element of our experience in work and art and imagination be consigned to non-creation, or to the non-divine. Faith is a public matter, a cultural fact, and not an individual private refuge or a private revelation. It is a social communication. The revelation of God occurs in the rough and tumble of actual history, not merely in the inner domain of spirituality. Faith can never desert the visible for some disembodied realm.

In treasuring the visible, faith claims the world of the senses. It has eyes, just as it hears, tastes, and inhales the presence of God. It senses the mystery in realities of the world, in the symbols of its sacraments, in the form of its words, in the face of its neighbor.

The invisible comes to us through the visible as an icon of the One who is.

Both the experience of the senses and the creativity of imagination are integrated into the ecstasy of faith. Signs, symbols, sacraments, and the incarnation itself, all point beyond themselves to what transcends our world. Since faith is never a mere matter of having a good look at the visible, believers never simply see God—in themselves or others, or, for that matter, in the entire event of the universe. Nonetheless, the invisible domain is not unfelt; it too is experienced. The realm of the invisible stirs in the depths of our consciousness, in all the dynamics of knowing and loving, judging, deciding, and of relating to the other and to the whole. It turns our consciousness into conscience, and lifts that conscience to its ultimate height in the experience of being loved and of being called to share in the life of love: "No one has ever seen God; if we love one another, God lives in us, and his love is perfected in us" (1 Jn 4:12).

In other words, there is an interior dimension of creation. In that invisible *within*, God's Spirit is manifest in our becoming aware both of our own ecstatic selfhood, and of creation as a whole. Creation is going on, both in the scientist's understanding the universe and in the physical universe itself; both in the artist's self-expressive activity and in the objective work of art; both in the mind finding meaning and in the reality it means; both in the silence of the mystic and in inspired words of faith and devotion; both in the integrity of good conscience and in the good deeds that are done.

In other words, creation is not just "already out there"; it is in the "in here," in the creativity of human consciousness, in all the modes of its loving, praying, exploring, acting, and communicating.

In this way, creation occurs as the *visible* becomes conscious of itself in the *invisible* reality of mind and heart and spirit; and as this *invisible* expresses itself in the *visible* domain of the material, public, social world. Adoration of the Creator leads to a truly bodily indwelling in the wonder of creation: matter and spirit, senses and mind, the external and the interior, are all related as each participates in the one created universe.

To conclude: faith lives in an awareness of everything as sheer gift. Thanking becomes the condition of true thinking. Our creative thinking and acting, in all the loving and doing, all participate in God's creation. The creativities of mind and heart, of eye and hand, of word and art, communicate in the unfolding of what is coming to be.

To believe in the Creator of all is to offer a fundamental praise to God. The divine Spirit is at work in the scientist and the scholar, in the inspired productions of the artist, in the contemplative and the mystic; most of all, in the ethical activity of good men and women working together in love and justice, to make the world both a human place and a biosphere cherishing the inherited diversity of all life.

To be part of creation and to adore the Creator is both a gift and a responsibility; for we live in the wonder of existing and acting and belonging in the universe God is making.

9

THE ONE LORD, JESUS CHRIST

We believe in one Lord, Jesus Christ ...

WE BELIEVE IN ...

In this second article, by far the longest, the creed cuts to its explicitly Christian core. Against the horizon of one original source of all things, faith recognizes this other "One" who has uniquely come forth, Jesus Christ, the only Son, our Lord. The infinite source of life engenders an Other, and eternally communicates itself. The Father pours his being into the Son, in the ecstasy of love. The silence of God utters itself in the Word. The darkness of "inaccessible light" radiates in "the light of the world." Faith comes to a moment of *reprise*. Our sense of the all-originating Father, the source of "all that is," is now refocused in the mystery of Jesus Christ.

If the first article nourishes the liturgical movement of *eucharistia*—thanksgiving and praise—the second bears on the moment of *anamnesis*, of remembering and calling to mind that second One who nourishes us with himself in the food and drink of the eucharist: the one Lord, Jesus Christ.

It is not so much a matter of passing from mystery to clarity, but of registering a new depth and vitality in the original mystery. In uttering its most precious name, Jesus Christ, the creed draws faith into a deeper darkness: "it is to your advantage that I go away" (Jn 16:7). But in the gift of the Paraclete, the witness and

confirmer of faith, faith comes to share in God's own consciousness of identity and communion: "no one knows the Son except
the Father" (Mt 11:27), just as "no one can say 'Jesus is Lord'
except by the Holy Spirit" (1 Cor 12:3).

Jesus does not somehow replace the one God. He is rather the
divine self-expression in which the one God is revealed to the
world. Christ is the point where "I will be who I will be" has
appeared personally among us. In the one Lord, Jesus Christ, the
infinite reality of God becomes intimately invocable.

In its schematic manner, the creed condenses the great sweep
of biblical rhetoric celebrating the reality of Christ. The scriptures
unfold in three great arcs of meaning: of fulfillment, of participation, and of universal extension (cf. Joseph Sittler).

First, Christ is a fulfillment. In him, God is expressed and
present in an irreversible and culminating manner. The "many and
various ways" of God's communication through the prophets has
reached its climax "in these last days" in the coming of the Son
(Heb 1:1–2). The Word, the Light, true God from true God,
becomes flesh and dwells among us. In the Father's giving of the
Son, divine love gives what is its very own for our salvation. And
as "Lord," Jesus receives the divine name that is above all names
(Phil 2:9). The first "incarnation" of the Word in all creation now
culminates as that Word comes "to what was his own" (Jn 1:11),
to be incarnate in our humanity.

The second great arc of scriptural meaning bears on the
unique inclusiveness of the mystery of Christ Jesus. By dwelling in
him, we dwell in God. By participating in him, believers
participate in the divine life. No one can come to the Father but
by him. We are members of his body and branches of the living
vine. In the language of an ultimate love, faith is embodied in
eating his flesh and drinking his blood, in breathing his Spirit, in
being baptized into his death and resurrection (Rom 6:3 f.). Jesus,
crucified and risen, is the way, the truth, and the life (Jn 15:4 f.).

Thirdly, faith finds in Christ a new and universal expansion
(Jn 1; Col 1; Eph 1; Heb 1): through him, all things were made.
Christ is not inserted into our world as some kind of major factor;
rather, the totality of creation is englobed in him to find its

deepest coherence and direction: he is "before all things")
Col 1:17) and all things find their goal in him. He is the alpha and
the omega of love's alphabet (Rev 22:13).

Thus the Word made flesh is the great poem of the almighty
Poet, the maker of all things. In the story of Jesus—of his
existence, conception, life, death, resurrection, and ascension into
heaven—the divine artist expresses the Word of life in the world.
Though the creed does not attempt to convey all these riches in its
language, it makes a space, as it were, in which the Gospel
narratives can be heard in the most telling manner. The confession
of the one Lord, Jesus Christ, is connected with the phrases
preceding it. Belief in the *one* Lord is referred back to belief in the
one God, just as confessing God as Father looks ahead to the One
he engenders, the only Son, the Father's most personal
communication and self-expression. The awesome almighty
character of the Father is brought down to earth in the humble
Lordship of Jesus. Heaven and earth, all that is, the visible and
invisible, are now condensed into the dimensions of the Word
made flesh. The "We believe" awakens to its original dependence
on the *We* of the Father and the Son.

We can now move on to the particular words and phrases of
this article.

ONE LORD, JESUS CHRIST

Jesus Christ is the one Lord in reference to the one God, not only
as the unique personal communication of this one God, but as
unifying the one divine creation as a universe of grace: "[The
Father has] set forth in Christ ... a plan for the fullness of time, to
gather up all things in him, things in heaven and things on earth"
(Eph 1:9–10). He is *one* also as the one way into the divine
communitarian life: "so that they may be one as we are one" (Jn
17:11). In his particular uniqueness Christ is the focus of all the
unifying activity of the one God:

> There is one body and one Spirit, just as you were called
> to the one hope of your calling, one Lord, one faith,
> one baptism, one God and Father of all, who is above
> all and through all and in all. (Eph 4:4–6)

Our Lord is one, then, as unifying all things as the unique culmination of God's communication to the world: "Long ago God spoke to our ancestors in many and various ways by the prophets, but in these last days he has spoken to us by a Son" (Heb 1:1–2). Because Christ is uniquely God's way to us, he is uniquely our way to God: "No one comes to the Father except through me" (Jn 14:6).

This one way of Christ does not disrupt creation or set believers apart from it. Faith means indwelling creation in its unique coherence in this one Lord: "in him all things hold together" (Col 1:17). To believe in this one Lord is to indwell a creation unified in Christ in a radically original manner: "All things came into being through him, and without him not one thing came into being" (Jn 1:3).

Not only is the one Christ implied in the origin and coherence of creation, the Son is also the direction and fulfillment of all that is. Reality is Christ-orientated in its deepest being: for in him has been revealed "… a plan for the fullness of time, to gather up all things in him, things in heaven and things on earth" (Eph 1:10). The generative powers of creation converge in the reality of this one Lord. As the traditional Advent antiphon from the Roman Liturgy has it, "Let the earth be open and bud forth the savior" (*aperiatur terra et germinet salvatorem*). For Christ is brought forth within the created world; he is "the firstborn of all creation … all things have been created through him and for him" (Col 1:15–16).

The uniqueness of Christ as origin, form, and goal of all creation does not mean that faith in him must result in a rigid exclusivism. Confessing Christ as the one Lord does not permit us to absolutize our present, partial apprehension of the oneness he embodies and actualizes. He so fills "all things" that the divine scope of what God is bringing forth in Christ remains immeasurably more than the tiny span of our present experience. To believe in Christ is to be ultimately related to everything and everyone. Thus, he is the Word, the *Logos*, provoking the dialogue, the *dialogos*, of unity, love, and meaning: "I have other sheep that do not belong to this fold. I must bring them also, and they will listen to my voice" (Jn 10:16). Especially today, there can be no authentic confession of Christ as the one Lord, as the one Word of God, unless in the context of the ever larger conversation taking place between God and the whole of humanity, and among human beings themselves in their search for what is ultimately true and good in existence: "In my Father's house there are many dwelling places" (Jn 14:2).

In a quite genuine sense, then, faith's confession of Christ as the *one* Lord is provisional; it is looking to completion. It is not a denial of the uniqueness of Christ to recognize that the ultimate gracious form of "all in Christ" has not yet been realized. To believe is always to anticipate a greater depth and breadth in the unity of everything and everyone in him: "in Christ God was reconciling the world to himself" (2 Cor 5:19). Faith must be busy as a reconciling love if it is to treasure the unique Word. The uniqueness of the *one* Lord is always provoking a greater unity.

While we have been emphasizing the unifying influence and action of the one Christ, Church teaching also underscores the fact that Jesus Christ is also one in himself. In him the divine and the human are united, so that he is "one person in two natures." In the one Lord, Jesus Christ, the divine finds its self-expression in the human; and the human finds its fulfillment and ultimate blessing in the divine. He is neither a divine person hiding behind a human face, nor a human person adopted into divine fellowship. He is God truly among us, God rendered invocable, God expressed and available to the eyes and ears and touch and taste of faith. In a way that neither reduces God nor destroys our humanness, the infinite distance between God and creation is bridged. The same One is truly God and truly human. In this sense he is "the man," the Human One, the ultimate form of the humanity God is bringing forth.

True, biblical presentations of Christ's uniqueness, and of the oneness and the unifying action associated with it, employ many more terms than are present in the creed. For example, it is possible to read the Gospel story on three levels. First, and most obviously, it is the story of Jesus, a human being, a man with a name, a history, a geographical and political setting, who was born, ate and drank, grew weary and disappointed, had friends, spoke a particular language, and who was finally killed on a particular date. On this level, he is a unique individual, among the billions that make up the human species.

Speaking more historically, Jesus of Nazareth was a man of remarkable humanity. His ability to make God real, to dramatize, in word and deed, his basic message of the imminent reign of God, his ethical teaching and the brilliance of his imagination, the tragedy of his execution, and the impact he has had on human history, place him among the classical figures of civilization—a unique human person.

The creed, while implying the first level in a number of ways, makes no mention of this second level; indeed, you might wonder how it could, given its schematic brevity. However, the creed does concentrate on a third level of the biblical data, that of the mystery of Jesus. Grounding the confession of Jesus as God's divine Son is his singular authority and sense of mission, both stemming from his unique relationship to the one he invokes so intimately as "my Father." The one God enters so intimately into his sense of identity, and so total is his sense of being from and for God, as Son of the Father, that the scriptures and subsequent liturgical and doctrinal confessions of the Church articulate the inner logic of faith by confessing him as divine in his radical identity. No human categories are sufficient to describe who, ultimately, he was and is.

Further, the creed unfolds in a certain sequence in its articulation of the saving significance of Jesus Christ: he is eternally begotten of the Father; all things are made through him; he comes down from heaven to be incarnate, born of the Virgin Mary through the power of the Spirit; he experiences his passion, death, and resurrection—and so on. In this sequence, the creed gives no hint of the order in which the sequence comes into the consciousness of faith. We are presented with faith full-blown, as it were, without any special indication of its genesis. Hence, a quick remark on that process can profitably be made.

At the outset, we must note that the scriptures imply three phases in their confession of the uniqueness of Christ, though seldom in an any ordered fashion. The first and most obvious phase is found in the Synoptic Gospels. They deal with the earthly life, origin, teaching, actions, relationships, and execution of Jesus of Nazareth—an account elsewhere referred to as what happened "in the days of his flesh" (Heb 5:7) and when "the Lord Jesus went in and out among us" (Acts 1:21). The second phase climaxes such narratives: it deals with the transformative event of the resurrection. Paul, for example, makes this starting point for his proclamation, with little explicit reference to the earlier phase. A third phase deals with the total significance of Christ: he is involved in the origin (protology) and end (eschatology) of all things. John's Gospel and Captivity Epistles provide the main texts here.

Now, in the genesis of faith, the resurrection of the Crucified One is the key transforming moment. Scholars differ on the degree to which the early disciples came to an explicit faith in Jesus as Son in the course of his earthly life. However, what is clear is that, in the resurrection, he came back to the disciples from a divinely transcendent realm, now embodying a life stronger than death and a love stronger than the power of any evil. In that revolutionary new awareness, the disciples were inspired to remember the deeper significance of Jesus' earthly life, and thus to understand fully, for the first time, who he was and what he was about. As the appearances of the Risen Lord re-arranged their understanding of how God was acting, the disciples looked both backward and forward to grasp the universal significance of Jesus. What happened in him involved the whole world. Hence, the path of faith to the assured confession of the uniqueness of Jesus is more complex than is suggested by the order of the creed. For in the genesis of faith, the resurrection of the Crucified One and the gift of the Spirit are far more important factors than a simple reading of the creed would suggest. The creed is shot through with a conviction of the reality of the resurrection: unless *that* had happened, unless that light had shone, unless they were absolutely certain about all *this*, Jesus would have been remembered, if at all, as one more good man who had been defeated by a world notoriously inhospitable to its prophets and reformers.

From beginning to end, the creed is an interpretation and condensation of the biblical witness. That original experience of the Risen One provoked a search for the right words and the right way to tell what had happened and what it meant. It inspired a long religious and theological development that, eventually, would be crystalized in the words of the creed. The sober, decisive wording of faith all too easily hides the ecstatic wonder at the heart of it. Jesus is this one Lord because all was revealed when the Crucified One was raised from the dead. Faith had met the Lord.

ONE *LORD*, JESUS CHRIST

The uniqueness of Jesus Christ is vividly expressed in his designation as Lord. John's Gospel climaxes when the risen Lord invites Thomas to touch his wounds, and the doubting disciple confesses, "My Lord and my God!" (Jn 20:28). No less startling, since it occurs as something so evidently presupposed, is Paul's exhortation to the Philippians to follow the example of Christ's self-giving love. The apostle adapts an early Christian hymn to his purpose, and concludes:

> Therefore God also highly exalted him and gave him the name that is above every name, so that at the name of Jesus every knee should bend, in heaven and on earth and under the earth, and every tongue should confess that Jesus Christ is Lord, to the glory of God the Father. (Phil 2:9–11)

The saving God of Isaiah, the unique Lord to whom "every knee shall bow, every tongue shall swear" (Isa 45:23), is now identified as Jesus, the Lord.

Probably the oldest and most condensed credal formula in the New Testament is "Jesus is Lord!" (cf. 1 Cor 8:6, 12:3; 2 Cor 4:5; Rom 10:9; Phil 2:11; Col 2:6). This simple confession epitomized the radically new consciousness of how God was now revealed in Christ. Drawn into a field of new life and divine presence, believers recognize Jesus for what he is: "no one can say 'Jesus is Lord' except by the Holy Spirit" (1 Cor 12:3). He inherits the sacred name of YHWH. The riddle of that name—"I will be who I will be" (Ex 3:14)—is finally resolved in this new burning bush, Jesus, the Crucified and Risen One.

Through the Lordship of Jesus, the Father exercises his divine reign within creation, and those who confess it are set in opposition to all other powers in this world, which contend for their allegiance. In a time of exuberant religiosity, Paul wrote to the Corinthians:

> Indeed, even though there may be many so-called gods
> in heaven or on earth—as in fact there are many gods
> and many lords—yet for us there is one God, the Father,
> from whom are all things and for whom we exist, and
> one Lord, Jesus Christ, through whom are all things and
> through whom we exist. (1 Cor 8:5–6)

Jesus, for the "We believe" of Christian faith, is "*our* Lord." He is not just a human figure lost in historical memory, a *he*, a *him* about whom we speak, but the *You* before whom faith lives. As our Lord, he is the medium and the mediator by whom we know the one God and our own ultimate identity and destiny. Nothing in all creation can compare with this Lord, since all else exists "through him." No one else can claim our allegiance, since he is the key to the whole meaning of our being: "through whom we exist." To believe is to choose him as Lord. Against all the forces of culture, society, economics, and politics that strive to wholly define our lives, Jesus is Lord, as the ultimate all-defining reality.

The confession of Jesus as Lord expresses both a radical engagement with the world and its values—all exists through him—and a critical reserve or "detachment," to use an older word, in the face of the world's demands and power. The oldest of Christian prayers, "Come, Lord Jesus!" (Rev 22:20), signals the ecstatic character of Christian existence—being in the world, yet not of it.

Consequently, to confess Jesus as our Lord is not to make him an idol. It is all too possible, as religious conflicts show, to project onto him the murderous burden of nationalistic aspirations or to use him as the legitimation of political ideologies of the left or right (usually the latter?). In contrast, he is the icon of the subversive reconciling love of God, not as congealing our experience into narrowness and exclusivity, but as opening our awareness to the suffering reality of our neighbor and to the needs of society. Like Thomas, only by touching the wounds of the one who gives himself for the life of the world do we acknowledge him as Lord. In imitating his washing of the disciples' feet, we are introduced into the social meaning of the kind of Lordship he exercises: "if I, your Lord and Teacher, have washed your feet, you also ought to wash one another's feet" (Jn 13:14). Such a Lordship redefines the meaning of power and of social relationships.

Moreover, the Lordship of Jesus does not impose an imperial measure on human time. God's patience has time for the whole of history. It does not hurry to have itself vindicated in premature glory. It respects God's acceptance of the ambiguity and incompleteness of our human condition. On the other hand, believers should have no desire to defer, either through dread or calculation, the ultimate realization of Christ's Lordship. There is room for a holy kind of impatience: "*Marana tha!* Our Lord, come!" (1 Cor 16:22).

In making space and time for the whole of history, Christ's Lordship is totally at the service of the Father's saving design. It works toward the point of perfect reconciliation between God and creation. In contending against all self-assertive modes of barricading human existence against the grace and mercy of God, this Lord opens creation to its real destiny. In this scheme of things, the lethal power of death is the last to go. As long as death threatens, mortal beings will cling to power, possessions, and fame, and all other forms of spurious immortality. But the Crucified One is risen. In him death is transformed into a final surrender to the creative love of God; the whole of creation is summoned home to its deathless glory in God:

> Then comes the end, when he hands over the kingdom
> to God the Father, after he has destroyed every ruler and
> every authority and power. For he must reign until he
> has put all his enemies under his feet. The last enemy to
> be destroyed is death … When all things are subjected
> to him, then the Son himself will also be subjected to

the one who put all things in subjection under him, so
that God may be all in all. (1 Cor 15:24–28)

To believe in Christ as Lord is to live in a time of essential
fulfillment. St John of the Cross writes, "When he gave us ... his
Son, who is one Word, he spoke everything to us, once and for all,
in that one Word. There is nothing further for him to say." The
great mystic imagines the Father speaking these words:

> "This is my beloved Son, with whom I am well pleased;
> listen to him." I have already told you all things in my
> Word. Fix your eyes on him alone, because in him I have
> spoken and revealed all. Moreover, in him you will find
> more than you ask or desire ... Hear him, because I
> have no more faith to reveal or anything to manifest. If
> I spoke in former times it was to promise Christ. And if
> they questioned me, their requests were steps along the
> road to want Christ and hope for him in whom they
> were to find all that is good. (*The Ascent of Mount
> Carmel*, book 2, chapter 22, quoted in *The Divine
> Office*, I, E. J. Dwyer, Sydney, 1974, pp. 78–79)

Still, we are not dealing with a nameless cosmic principle or
religious abstraction. Our Lord has a human name. He is ...

JESUS CHRIST

"Jesus" is, of course, the Latin form of a common Hebrew name,
Yeshua (or Joshua), meaning "He will save." This point is not lost
on Matthew when, in his account of Jesus' origins, he has the angel
saying to Joseph about Mary, his betrothed, and the child who is to
be born, "She will bear a son, and you are to name him Jesus, for
he will save his people from their sins" (Mt 1:21). Thereafter, in the
Gospel and in the whole of Christian life, that name provokes the
most elemental of all prayers, "Save us ... " (cf. Mt 8:25, etc.).

To name the Lord in this human way underscores the reality of
the incarnation. The Word of God uniquely embodied in him is a
person in human history, located geographically, speaking and

spoken to in a particular language, and in the context of a particular culture and political situation. It means, too, that this name is "the holy name," invoked in the most condensed and personal form of faith. It expresses the saving significance of this man from Nazareth who bore this name and lived out its meaning. In all the ways he spoke and acted, lived and suffered, and continues to be present to the community of faith, Jesus is "he who saves." Invoked in that name, Jesus is the final, gracious translation of YHWH, "I will be who I will be" (Ex 3:14). Peter, preaching his first sermon, quotes the prophet Joel, "everyone who calls on the name of the Lord shall be saved" (Acts 2:21). He exhorts his hearers to repentance and to "be baptized ... in the name of Jesus Christ" (Acts 2:38). He demonstrates how healing comes to the sick by "the name of Jesus Christ" (Acts 3:6, 4:10), and "there is no other name under heaven given among mortals by which we must be saved" (Acts 4:12). Indeed, "signs and wonders are performed through the name of your holy servant Jesus" (Acts 4:30).

Through this "holy name," then, the saving presence of God is invoked. Because Jesus is a proper name, it serves to remind faith of its origins in history. For Christian faith is not primarily based on a principle of thought or action or even on inspired writings, but on a person: a historically identifiable "he," a "you" who can call us each by name even as we address him. Christian faith means living a convivial relationship with this God-given, humanly-named other. Whatever the overwhelming glory of God, we reach to its heart in meeting such a person with such a name:

> Then a cloud overshadowed them, and from the cloud
> there came a voice, "This is my Son, the Beloved; listen
> to him!" Suddenly when they looked around, they saw
> no one with them any more, but only Jesus.
> (Mk 9:7–8)

This name, Jesus, includes a larger sweep of history when it comes to be linked in a personal manner with the more general title, "Christ."

JESUS *CHRIST*

First, the word itself: the Greek word *christos* translates the Hebrew *Messiah*, meaning the "anointed," one ritually designated to a sacred office, as with Israel's priests, kings, and often prophets. Anointing with oil is an ancient and widespread symbolic gesture.

More particularly, the Christ–Messiah emerges in the history of Israel as the special bearer of the hopes of God's people, a person or perhaps a group uniquely anointed by the Spirit of God to bring salvation. Understandably, given the oppressions and sufferings of Israel's history, the messianic figure was imagined as marvelously fulfilling the expectations of the people. There were overtones of political victory and the decisive vindication of Israel's hopes when God and his people would come finally into their own.

In the Jewish milieu of Jesus' life, inevitable questions arose as to just who he was and what he was about. The Gospels present the meaning of Christ as something of a riddle. It was a catalyst for both questioning and confessing the identity of Jesus (Mk 8:28 f., 14:61 f.), tending to provoke the spiritual struggle out of which a decision to follow him could be made. While early preaching told of "how God anointed [i.e., christened] Jesus of Nazareth, ... how he went about doing good and healing all who were oppressed by the devil, for God was with him" (Acts 10:38), this seemingly simple narrative presupposed a kind of decoding of the meaning of the "Christ." Those formed in the deep consciousness of Israel's faith—and this surely includes Jesus himself—were under no impression that the Messiah could be a simply glorious, triumphant figure. The "suffering servant" prophecies of Isaiah (50–53) could hardly permit that. The increasing reality of conflict prevented Jesus from making any identification of himself with a glorious Messiah. The eventual fact of the cross—the foolishness of God that was to be such a scandal to the Jews, such a folly to the Greeks (1 Cor 1:23), and, incidentally, such a subversion of the imperial world-view—became a divine irony on all human pretension: "Oh, how foolish you are, and how slow of heart to believe all that the prophets have declared! Was it not necessary that the Messiah should suffer these things and then enter into his glory?" (Lk 24:25–26). In the light of the resurrection of the Crucified One, the true meaning of Jesus as the Christ was revealed—not as triumphant in human power, but as serving in the vulnerability of the properly divine power of love. He neither excludes nor condemns his enemies, but includes them in a universe of mercy: "Father, forgive them; for they do not know what they are doing" (Lk 23:34).

By joining the name Christ to that of Jesus, the memory of faith retains its sense of the riddle of the divine name: "I am who I will be." God will be revealed on his own terms and in his own way. Each of the two biblical forms of his name, "Jesus Christ" and "Christ Jesus," make a point. As Jesus Christ, he is this man from Nazareth, this Jesus, who lived, suffered, and died on the cross, now revealed as the all-inclusive mystery of salvation: the Christ. When confessed as "Christ Jesus," he is Christ, the Risen Lord, present to all the churches, but always identified as the one who was crucified, Jesus of Nazareth.

In the history of those who accepted Jesus as Christ, an original nickname stuck: his followers were called "Christians." By committing themselves to the folly of following him, they committed themselves to the way of his vulnerable love. They too would have an anointing of the Spirit and share in his death and resurrection. The various sacramental anointings in the rituals of faith (such as baptism, confirmation, ordination, and the anointing of the sick) are designed to express this point.

More poignantly, the designation of Jesus as Christ places Christian faith in its essential relationship with Israel. There can be no Christian faith save by sharing the hopes of Israel regarding the one true God and the promised Christ. In the words of Jesus, "salvation is from the Jews" (Jn 4:22). The nations are the wild olive shoot grafted in "to share the rich root of the olive tree" (Rom 11:17). Yet, as Christians believe that the Christ has come in the crucified and risen Jesus, while the Jews of today still await his appearance, conflicts emerge; not without the sad history of animosity, separation, and mutual recrimination. To what degree a more God-centered faith in both Christianity and Judaism alike can be reconciled in a shared waiting for the full glory of the Christ to appear, how much dialogue might now be possible after the terrifying conflicts and bitter recriminations of the past, are questions now reverently asked in the grace of the present.

He is, indeed, Jesus the Jew. For Christians to deny or underplay that fact is to incur the peril of denying their own history, and God's action within it. Similarly, for Jewish believers to ignore the witness of Jesus, their fellow Jew, is to risk denying their own hope-filled history. Only in patience, forgiveness, and prayer can a new era of reconciliation occur, and God be left free to act according to the name "I am who I will be."

10

FROM THE HEART OF GOD

———

... the only Son of God,
eternally begotten of the Father,
God from God, Light from Light,
true God from true God,
begotten, not made,
of one Being with the Father.
Through him all things were made.

After naming the personal object of faith—the one Lord, Jesus Christ—the creed now elaborates the full truth of Jesus' identity. Everything that Jesus is—in the events of his life, death, resurrection, ascension, in his glorification at God's right hand as judge and ruler of the world—is tied back into the depths of the divine reality itself. Who Jesus is in time is who he is before all ages, in the eternal life of God. The divine mystery can be so personal in its communication, so intimate in its self-giving, because it has such a self to give. In generating the Son from all eternity, the Father can give what is most intimate to his own life, for the life of the world. Hence, the creed confesses the one Lord, Jesus Christ, as God's ...

ONLY SON
How God has a Son, how such a generation occurs in the eternal vitality of God, is elaborated in our reflections on the phrases

that follow. For the moment, we simply stress that all the communications of God to creation, all the ways in which human beings rejoice in a filial intimacy with God—as God's sons and daughters—point back to an original self-communication in the divine life itself. The God of our faith is neither eternally alone nor eternally lifeless. Not alone, since there is the beloved Other. Not lifeless, because this beloved Other originates in the eternal vitality of Love's communication. The Father generates the Son. In such clearly metaphorical terms, a divine vitality of unstinted, eternal self-giving is implied. The very life of God is communication.

ETERNALLY BEGOTTEN OF THE FATHER

The New Testament interprets the whole history of God's dealing with creation as culminating in the coming of the Son among us. The time of Christian faith follows, a time for realizing the extent of the gift of God, and of extending such a realization into every aspect of our existence. Whereas God allows for such time as essential to his purpose, time itself is held together and directed to its end by the timeless origination of the Son in the depth of divine life. An eternal begetting is at the heart of all that happens in history.

For the creed to acknowledge this eternal generation of the Son by the Father is to affirm that, through Jesus Christ, we are being drawn into God's own life. The history of faith does not depend primarily on what happened a long time ago. Present in the passage of time is the timeless mystery of God's living reality. All that God is for us in time is essentially a prolongation into time of what God is in and for God's very self: the Father brings forth the Son, and the Son lives from and for the Father. While time entropically erodes and diminishes the events of even the greatest significance, faith refreshes its vitality from the eternal vitality of God present in and present to its every moment. Every instant of our present is filled with the presence of the infinite liveliness of God's self-giving love. There is no time in which God is not the Living One, eternally begetting the Son, in the unity of the Spirit.

To such an understanding, time, and the world in time, comes into being through an eternal, all-pervading, divine vitality. Hence the creed underscores two aspects of its basic truth. First, the temporal sequence of the Word/Son becoming flesh, in his human growth and deeds and words, in his cross and resurrection, does not mean that God is contained in human history or in the larger universal process. Rather, the divine "procession" (to use a technical word designating the manner in which the Son and Spirit originate within God) of the Son from the Father is the reason why there is any temporal process at all. The abiding vitality of God's fathering love contains time together with all its processes and dynamics. The Son is sent ("mission" is here another technical term) into the world, and offered to the world for what he is, in his eternal identity. His entry into the world as a human being in time does not add something essentially new to the being and life of God. Rather, the incarnation is the eternal vitality of God's self-communication overflowing into time. The radical identity of Jesus as Son, eternally begotten of the Father, is not defined by time, but contains time, and makes time and history pregnant with divine meaning and direction.

This leads to a second point. The eternity of God's self-giving vitality is not opposed to time. The coming forth of the Son saves time from being a pointless succession of events, from being a slow, doomed winding down as the forces of entropy impose their laws. Through the incarnation of the eternal Son, time is radically personalized and made into a movement of grace. God has time for the world's unfolding. Our fragmented experience of time and history finds its inner consistency and direction in the original, time-transcending identity of the Son. Through Christ, our time participates in the eternal reality of God's life of communion. The life, death, and resurrection of the one Lord, Jesus Christ, are the temporal unfolding of the character of "the only Son of God, eternally begotten of the Father": "So now, Father, glorify me in your own presence with the glory that I had in your presence before the world existed" (Jn 17:5).

The human life of the Son inscribes into time its original and final meaning. Being above time, being the self-giving event at the origin of time, God alone can have time for the whole unfolding of history and the universe. When the Word becomes flesh, God becomes what is other in the extreme, to enfold that other into the life of divine communion. The life of God opens into human history. Time becomes the carrier of a timeless life; each moment is filled with an eternal vitality:

> Blessed be the God and Father of our Lord Jesus Christ,
> who has blessed us in Christ with every spiritual
> blessing in the heavenly places, just as he chose us in
> Christ before the foundation of the world to be holy
> and blameless before him in love. (Eph 1:3–4)

The history of Jesus is the temporal enactment of God's eternal self-expression in the Son. In the freedom of love, the eternal vitality of love reaches into history "for us ... and our salvation." The following phrases of the creed take us more deeply into the meaning of the eternal communion that God ever actually *is*.

BEGOTTEN OF THE FATHER

This phrase and those that follow testify to a great learning experience in the Church agitated by conflicts surrounding the Arian controversy. Arius had maintained that the one God was intrinsically alone; there could be no sharing in what God essentially is. Necessarily the Son had to be created, even though he was to be ranked as the highest of creatures. For Arius, anyone coming forth from God had to be less than God; made by the supreme maker, a part of creation. Against this Greek philosophical notion of the solitary, transcendent God presupposed by Arius, the Council of Nicaea (325) resolutely affirmed the communicative, convivial reality of the one God. The council maintained an eternal self-communication within God. God could give his only Son because God truly had such a Son to give.

So the creed insists that the Son is truly begotten of the Father. God is essentially communicative and essentially a communion. The Father is the eternal God bringing forth his divine reality in the other, his only Son, and relating to this other in the Spirit of self-giving love.

Therefore the words of the creed, "begotten of the Father,"are chosen to oppose any sense of the Son as a creation in time: "begotten," as opposed (as we will see below) to "made." In the realm of an intra-divine origination and communion, the generation of the Son is a divine procession, a unique origination that is proper to the divine life itself.

How can we speak of this divine process of self-communication? Here, as elsewhere in speaking of God, we have to use human analogies. Implied in the human metaphors of fatherhood and sonship is the *metaphor* of generation or begetting. Following the ancient scholastic analysis, we say that one living being begets another when the offspring immediately originates from the other in an identical nature. Hence a rock does not beget moss, since the moss is *living* and the rock is not. Nor do we say that the animal body begets hair or fur, since there is *no identical nature* implied. Nor do we say that a grandparent begets a grandchild, since there is no *immediate* relationship as with parent and child; it is literally a generation removed. But when a living child immediately comes forth from a living parent in the same nature, we can say that the father begets and the child is begotten.

Hence the metaphor of generation, as opposed to that of mere making or producing, is favored. In the procession of the Son, we have one living reality immediately originating from another in the likeness of nature. Hence, a divine begetting. But a problem remains: generation pertains to terrestrial biology. Procreation is the result of a sexual conception. Understanding the generative reality of God, therefore, demands a deft use of analogy, since God is not a species of biological life and is outside male or female genderization. Early in Christian thought (in the writings of Justin Martyr, for instance) such analogical thinking began to be explored. The generation of the Son was clarified in terms of the divine speaking of the Word, as an inner word, a spiritual conception. God conceives of all that God is and can be in the Word. When this word is understood as God's perfect self-utterance, theology can throw some light on how the Son is "generated," "conceived," or "begotten" by God. Representatives of this classic line of Christian thinking are Augustine,

Athanasius, and, in the Middles Ages, Thomas Aquinas. In such theologies, the Son/Word is God's perfect self-expression and self-communication, pertaining to God's most intimate self-possession. In Christ as Son, God is for us what God is in the divine reality itself: "If we are faithless, he remains faithful—for he cannot deny himself" (2 Tim 2:13).

Hence, "begotten of the Father" in the creed implies that the Father is self-expressively God, and that the Son is God self-expressed. Thus, the way is opened for a notion of the Holy Spirit as that which enables such self-expression, and as that which results from it—the Spirit as God's self-possession in infinite joy and unity.

God from God

As the complete self-expression of God, the Son is "God from God." Jesus as Son has a divine origin. He is uniquely from the Father. From this intuition arises one of the most provocative insights of classic trinitarian theology. The person of the Son consists in a pure relationship. As such he is the revelation of the relational character of all personhood. The Son, being "from and for the Father in the Spirit of love," draws all that is made—above all the whole of personal creation—into his relational life. In the Son, we are sons and daughters of God.

The divine reality emerges as one of communion and relationship. The divine persons are distinct, not as being different gods—for there is only one God—but as pure relationships to each other. Trinitarian life comes to be understood as a realm of vital interrelationships. Each divine person is in the others, and all are in each, since the identity of each implies relationship to the others. Hence the ancient name, *perichoresis*, a "dancing around together," a "circuminsession," a mutual indwelling, a vital co-inherence in reciprocal yielding and surrender. The consciousness of God unfolds in that intimate communal vitality in which each divine person yields to the other in the joy of one divine life.

Light from Light

In contrast to the more austere theological language preceding and following this phrase, one of the most ancient symbols of

God is now invoked. The symbol of light is employed in a deliberately metaphorical language colored, we must assume, by all its associations with the baptismal and paschal liturgies. The verbal use of the metaphor of light and the symbolic use of light and flame evokes one of the most primal experiences of God: "God is light and in him there is no darkness at all" (1 Jn 1:5). God dwells "in unapproachable light" (1 Tim 6:16), in contrast to glimpses of the mystery experienced in the chiaroscuro of our journey through time.

The only Son is, like the Father, a source of light, not merely a reflection or a created mirror. He is himself the light (Jn 8:12; Lk 2:32). For the whole of the New Testament, God is light because God is love. The incarnate Son radiates in this way the "love-light" of God's gracious presence to creation. The suggestive power of the language of light is exemplified in the words of St Athanasius:

> The sun and its brightness are two things, but there is
> one light, born of the sun, which, with its brightness,
> illuminates the whole universe. Similarly the Son's
> divinity is also that of the Father, and so there is but
> one divinity ... Therefore, because they are one, and
> because the divinity itself is also one, what is said of the
> Father is also said of the Son, except the name Father.
> Thus the Son is called God; and the Word was God; he
> is also called omnipotent ... Lord ... Light.*

TRUE GOD FROM TRUE GOD

The creed now brings us back from the evocative power of imagination to the gravity of making a judgment of truth. In the measure faith holds to Love's self-expression in the Word, to Love's self-giving in the Son, be it in prayer, liturgical symbolism or doctrine, it is concerned with the truth. Just as the Father is being true to himself in the Son and Word, Christian faith must be true to itself in confessing Jesus as "true God from true God." Five points may be suggested in this regard:

* Athanasius, *De Decretis Nic. Syn.*, 20, MG 25, 452, quoted in B. Lonergan, *The Way to Nicaea*, Westminster Press, Philadelphia, 1976, pp. 100 f.

First, the Son is true God from the true God. The God of faith is the one true God, neither a mythic deity nor a religious fantasy. All the symbols and metaphors of faith work in the experience of faith to lead to the reality of what God truly is.

Secondly, Jesus Christ is true God from this true God. He is not just a human symbol of the divine, nor the occasion of speaking imaginatively about the divine in human terms. Christian faith affirms that in Christ, in fact and in actuality, it is contacting the genuine reality of God: Jesus is the truth of God. In him, in his saving sacrificial love, the real God is being true to what God actually is. God is truly self-expressed in the person, life, death, and resurrection of Jesus.

Thirdly, in daring to use this word "true" in its confession, faith is responding to the demand to be true to itself. The integrity of Christian faith begins and ends in its conviction that the one true God is truly revealed in the one Lord, Jesus Christ. Whatever the imperatives of dialogue in the inter-faith world of today, they do not dissolve the absolute conviction of Christian faith into relativity. Learning from and learning with followers of other religions cannot mute, in any way, the Christian sense of fundamental truth. In fact, because of the absolute truth of what faith holds and celebrates, dialogue with believers of other faiths is demanded. For Christ is not *a* truth but *the* truth. This conviction implies no arrogant exclusivity. While Christian integrity must affirm the truth of Christ as the revelation of God and the savior of the world, who among us can pretend to understand the full meaning of what God has done in Christ? In no period of history can believers so absolutize their particular understanding of the divine Word as to claim that they have exhausted the depth and extent of the incarnation. Nonetheless, before faith is dialogue with others, it is dialogue with God, receptive to what has been declared in all its uniqueness. The creed allows for no ambiguity in its confession because the Word of God is not ambiguous: "true God from true God."

Fourthly, the truth in question here concerns the objectivity of Christian realism. The realities affirmed by faith provoke the working of mind and intellect: by believing we come to understand.

For faith discloses new data about what and who God really is; it frees the intelligence to pursue the meaning of what has been so given—in terms of God, of the self, and of the whole of creation; it inspires the tasks of Christian reflection and the exploration of reasons that make the assent of faith intelligent, creative, and clear. Faith is beholden to reality; it deals with what *is*.

Because faith aims to affirm what is the "really real," Christian beliefs are necessarily a public statement. They constitute a cultural position. To believe is to take a stand in history, both supported and burdened with a sense of the ultimate truth of God. Only a concern for the truth and the deepest sense of reality can be a sufficient foundation for the unity of the Church and, in the long run, for the continuing creativity of civilization itself. If the judgments of faith are true, they are very true; and to deny them is to settle for a mutilated and distorted existence.

Should the truth of Christian faith be rejected, it is some consolation to the believer if it is rejected for the right reasons—not because its essential judgments are attenuated, confused, or fudged in some way. In affirming that Christ is "true God from true God," faith in fact rejects any notion of the Son as a mere appearance or reflection or symbol or model of the divine, in such a way that the genuine reality of God is left unknown or finally unknowable. The truth-bearing reality of faith's judgments transcends all human models of reality to assert, however reverently and in whatever darkness, what is genuinely true of God. The intent of such Christian realism takes faith beyond images, beyond concepts and words, to the divine reality itself. Faith is not about believing in myths, symbols, narratives, or metaphors, however much such expressions may figure in religious language. It is about believing in God as the ultimately and uniquely real, in response to the self-revelation of the divine in Christ.

Fifthly, faith not only demands that mind be true to itself, but welcomes the truth of the heart. The heart cannot rest content by resigning itself to the hopelessness of accepting that what we most value is at the mercy of what we most fear. The deepest feeling of the believing heart nourishes the assurance that love, truth, and goodness have to be stronger than evil and death. The human self is made to meet Someone who alone can be the heart's peace and fulfillment. In Christ, what we most deeply feel ourselves to be is welcomed and loved, healed and made whole; and so given a hope, a peace, and a joy not of this world. In Christ, the world itself appears as God's redeemed creation, destined for resurrection. The heart runs forward to the whole truth of Christ before our minds can catch up with it, or bring it to expression. In the language of the creed, "true God from true God," the heart finds words that it hardly dares to utter: we live in a universe of grace ... "and you will know the truth, and the truth will make you free" (Jn 8:32).

BEGOTTEN, NOT MADE

The Son who is truly God comes forth from the true God, not as a created reality, but in terms of a pure, undiminished self-communication. To be begotten means that the Son is the one into whom the Father has poured the fullness of divine being and love. In this relationship of giving and receiving, the Son is not less than the Father. The living communion of the Trinity is not modeled on finite or worldly instances of needy dependence. Being from and for the other in the divine case does not imply diminishment and need as in human patterns of experience. "Begotten, not made" is the language of divine fullness and ecstatic communion. God does not reside in infinite solitude and self-containment, but lives in self-giving and relationship.

Because the Son is not made like the rest of creation, because he is the perfect self-utterance of the Father, his generation is the primordial movement of life behind all creation. The "procession" of the Son from the Father is the cause, the form, and the goal of the whole creative process: "All things came into being through him" (Jn 1:3). The divine "fathering" is eternally presupposed in all divine making. That is to say that the existence of all creation, and of each one of us in that creation, is first of all conceived in the eternal Word. That timeless conception is realized in the time of creation, to be recognized in time when believers are gathered to confess that the Son is "begotten, not made"; and, as the creed will go on to add, "through him all things were made."

OF ONE BEING WITH THE FATHER

Because the Son is begotten, not made, he is not, compared with the Father, on a lower level. The relationships between them are symmetrical, on the same level, inherent in one realm of divine life—one in being, consubstantial. The emblematic word of the Council of Nicaea is here inserted, *homoousion*, literally "of the same stuff/substance," belonging to the same divine realm.

At the point where the creed sounds most philosophical, it is in fact breaking free from any purely philosophical notion of God. The Christian notion of God is not of an infinite, solitary, self-sufficient excellence, but the reality of a divine being-in-love, realized in self-giving and relationship. The primordial activity of God does not consist in exercising lordship over creation, but in its inner life of self-giving love. The Father communicates the fullness of divine being to the Son. From such original self-communication, all the gifts of God follow.

As one in being with the Father, the Son uniquely reveals what the Father is. Only through God's self-expression in the Son does faith know what God is like. In other words, "God" is not primarily a general religious notion, but the reality defined in reference to the Word made flesh. Since "our Lord Jesus Christ" is the living definition of what God means, the Christian sense of God does not start out with a cultural or philosophical definition of God, and then try to align the reality of Christ Jesus to such a conception. The controlling factor in our knowledge of God is not something extrinsic to Christian faith—for example, some religious or social presumption of what "God" is like. This can happen, of course, and it did happen in the classical ancient instance of Arius. He asserted that Christ as Son and Word *had* to be created because what was truly divine could not originate from another, could not become incarnate, could not suffer. Therefore, Christ had to be a creature, and the Son has to have a temporal beginning.

Against such a dis-incarnate, non-christological notion of God stands the great affirmation of the Council of Nicaea (325), now incorporated into the creed we are examing:

> We believe in one God, the Father, almighty, maker of
> all things visible and invisible. And in one Lord Jesus

Christ, the Son of God, begotten of the Father, only
begotten, that is, from the substance of the Father; God
from God, Light from Light, true God from true God,
begotten not made, of one substance with
(*homoousion*) the Father, through whom all things came
into being ... who, because of us and our salvation,
came down and became incarnate, becoming man,
suffered and rose again ...

Hence, Christ is, in person, not just a symbol of God, nor a man adopted in some way into a special religious relationship, but the very *self*-communication of the divine. God gives into the world, in a loving self-emptying, what is most intimate to the God-self, the beloved Son, as God from God and Light from Light. The implication is clear: God is self-giving in a way that limitlessly exceeds all human forms of self-giving. In Christ, God has not just done *something* for us, but is given and present as the divine *Someone*, the Son, the Word. God is self-expressed in the world in the way the divine truth is expressed to itself in the eternal life of the Trinity. The relationship of Jesus to the Father as it unfolds in time, from the wholeness of Jesus' heart and mind and soul and strength, is nothing but the enactment of who he is as the eternal Son. So, faith builds up its notion of the true God by overhearing, as it were, the eternal dialogue between the Father and the Son as it has extended into time and human history. The one who is begotten within the womb of the Trinity is begotten now in the womb of Mary.

While the creed accentuates the transcendent origin of the Son, Christ is not given to creation as something or someone foreign to it, as though from the outside. Therefore, the next phrase declares the intimate presence of Christ to all reality.

Through Him All Things Were Made

Once more the creed takes us to a limit. Contemporary science is increasingly familiar with how the cosmos is a totality of interconnected events in the great emergent process of the universe. The hologram, rather than the mechanism of the clock, most symbolizes our present sense of reality. In its relationships to the whole, in its participation in the all, in the interconnected, undular nature of all reality, each element of the universe is constituted. Today, the cosmos is holistically conceived. It is as though everything and everyone is active and present, one to the other, each to the all, the all to each.

But the creed does not let us stop there. We are led to affirm a primordial agency, an all-comprehending and fundamental meaning, in which the universe of all that is enjoys a basic consistency and ultimate direction. If the Father is Creator of all, then this *all*, the totality of all that is and is coming to be, is made through our Lord Jesus Christ, the only Son. In the divine self-expression of the Word, in that original "fathering forth" of God in the Son, in the incarnation of that Word, in the passion, death, and resurrection of the Son, in the final manifestation of this Son as judge of the living and the dead, "all things were made"—and are being made. Christ is the original and final form of the world's becoming.

Again, faith is led into its distinctive darkness. Its "catholicity" or "cath-holism"—openness to the all of everything and everyone in Christ—inspires a gradual, often painful awakening to the universal scope of the meaning of Christ. It grounds an all-inclusive hope destined to contend with all forms of power-driven totalitarianism. The twentieth century knows enough about the ideological pathologies of left or right, and about their lethal violence in trying to press history into a blank and hopeless uniformity. In contrast, the "all of Christ" allows for the full play of history, and the individuality and distinctiveness of each element and each person of God's creation. The gracious imagination of faith subverts all human efforts to reduce the meaning of our experience to all those "nothing buts" of, say, biochemical structures, genes, evolutionary processes, or social forces. Such "alls" and "nothing buts" do, of course, have their own partial and relative reality. They are certainly not excluded by faith's sense of the "all in Christ." But that original and final Christ-totality has to wait for its full evidence, when God is "all in all." In the meantime, that evidence exists only in the divine consciousness, not in our own. It is received only through faith. Faith lives, then, in a horizon of hope, waiting for the moment when its whole truth will out. It is left not with a theory, but an ever-expanding perception of the all-inclusive meaning of Christ. In the Crucified and Risen One, we are all dying to a self-enclosed particularity to rise to the self-surrendering co-existence of "all in Christ." In him, "heaven and earth," "the seen and unseen" of God's creation are condensed into the humanity of God, Christ, the Incarnate One.

In contemplating all in Christ, faith perceives the universe of things and processes and persons as conceived of by God in an eternal self-expression: true light from true light. In that light, the Father knows and loves the Son, and, in him, the whole of creation: the all of which we are a part is eternally conceived in the mind and heart of God.

Further, the all—in which we ourselves come to be—has a fundamental unity: an eternal divine meaning and all-containing divine love comprehends the universe as a uni-verse: everything is christened in the divine heart and shares in the filial identity of the Christ: "He himself is before all things, and in him all things hold together" (Col 1:17). From its beginning and in every stage of its emergence, the universe is geared to the incarnation as its focal point. Its many dyings and transformations participate in the paschal mystery of the Son's death and resurrection. The eucharist celebrates how "the fruit of the earth and the work of human hands" are transformed into the body and blood of Christ, nourishing faith into a sense of the divine totality of everything in Christ. The waters of baptism flow and wash with his life and healing and whole-making power.

This coherence of all in Christ makes the universe in its every element, energy, and consciousness ultimately relational. At the core of all reality is the supreme relationship that Christ personifies by being totally from and for the Father in the Spirit. Consequently, he is unreservedly "for us … and our salvation." This gives rise to faith's specific field of awareness—a relational universe. The trinitarian relationships that make God divine also structure the reality of the created world. To exist is to be related to the other—to be ecstatic, drawn out of ourselves, to live and die into the ultimately holy, the wholeness of God's creation in Christ.

Further, faith deals with the world as it actually is, in the whole groaning totality of its blessings, longings, and agonies. For there is evil, as there was in the garden of Genesis; though God does not cause evil, the patience of creative love takes time for the whole drama of human freedom to be played out. The cross is the enduring symbol of how God allows for the dreadful drama of human freedom, yet the love that gives itself in the Son is not defeated by human evil. Such love led Jesus to the utter vulnerability of the cross; though it sends him down to that "hell" of impotence and despair—to the point where we instinctively feel that God cannot touch us, where God is reduced to nothing (his descent into hell as the Apostles' Creed has it)—it does lead him out. He is "the first born of all creation." In the transformative moment of resurrection, the light of love proves stronger than any darkness we know.

Believing, however, does not mean being in possession of a final evidence. Surrender to the healing and unifying reality of Christ is always demanded. In him is embodied and shared the whole world in a state of transformation, of giving itself, in death and self-dispossession, for the all: "This is my body given up for you and for all."

Finally, faith in the universe created in Christ does not permit believers to exclude anyone or anything from the realm of God's love. Nothing and no one can be extruded from the promise of life. Again, the elegance of a beautiful vision is not the issue here. Nor is it a matter of constructing an optimistic system. The challenge consists in actually following Christ as the Way, in the energies of love and hope. In Christ, whatever the scandal of our apart-ness and enmities in this present time, faith turns into a hope that we will all ultimately belong together:

> Those who say, "I love God," and hate their brothers or
> sisters, are liars; for those who do not love a brother or
> sister whom they have seen, cannot love God whom they
> have not seen. (1 Jn 4:20)

Hence, the creed implicitly leads us from the vision of "all in Christ" into the world of social options. As believers, we must live out the interconnected totality of christened reality. To exist now is to be sons and daughters in the Son, to breathe his all-connecting Spirit, to adore the God who welcomes us into a home of many rooms. And it means to decide to live as if what we believe is really true, consenting to a truth that demands to be realized.

Once more we can emphasize that the whole universe is the cosmic incarnation of the Word. The historical fact of the incarnation in Jesus Christ discloses original and final dimensions of this mystery. St Athanasius ponders various metaphors. He envisages the Word as the soul animating the great body of the universe and as the one Word sung in the great polyphony of creation. Most of all, he stresses the christic wholeness of the world in terms of music. His words fittingly conclude this section:

> There is nothing existing or created that did not come into being and subsist in him and through him, as the theologian says, "In the beginning was the Word, and the Word was with God, and the Word was God. All things were made by him, and without him nothing was made."
>
> Just as a musician, tuning his lyre and skilfully combining bass and sharp notes, the middle and the others, produces a single melody, so the wisdom of God, holding the universe like a lyre, draws together the things in the air with those on earth, and those in heaven with those in the air, and combines the whole with the parts, linking them by his command and will, thus producing in beauty and harmony a single world and a single order within it, while the Word of God remains unmoved with the Father but by his intrinsic being moves everything as seems good to the Father. Everything according to its nature is given life and subsistence by him; and through him a wonderful and divine harmony is produced.*

* St Athanasius, *Against the Gentiles*, nn. 42–3, trans. by Robert W. Thompson, © Oxford University Press, 1971.

11
THE COMPASSION OF GOD

———

For us [all] men and for our salvation
he came down from heaven ...

FOR US ALL

Propter nos homines: this phrase must be translated in contemporary inclusive language, as in "for us all" or "for us human beings." For the creed, in expressing God's saving love in the broadest possible inclusiveness, is referring to the most fundamental solidarity existing among us as human beings, *homines*. Before we are defined in terms of political, cultural, national, racial, sexual, or even religious differences, we are, in the sight of God and one another, "we human beings," *nos homines*. In our human-ness we are beloved of God, as those for whom God is so lovingly *for*.

God's love for us in Christ affirms and enhances our solidarity with one another. Conscious of the inclusive scope of that love, the creed can say "we human beings" in the solidarity of hope. Yet the human race is more than the sum of its members if only for the reason that the divine Son himself, in the incarnation, has claimed membership in our history. The human story is no longer merely a tragic tale of defeats or a brilliant history of successes. The central historical fact is that our humanity has been met and accompanied in its journey through time by this one who is "for us" by being "with us," Emmanuel, God-with-us (Mt 1:23).

Beyond all the ways in which we have failed both individually and communally to be for one another, despite all manner of our being against one another—even on religious grounds—our Lord Jesus Christ, from beginning to end and in every moment, is radically and ultimately "for us."

Since "all things are made through him," Christ is the medium in which everything and everyone is most intimately and originally united—especially that human part of "all things" that can speak the word "we."

Christ's being "for us" reveals the intention of divine love to enfold us into the way the Father is "for" his only Son. The basic character of trinitarian life is to be limitlessly "for the other," in self-giving love. The way God is for the other within the trinitarian life is manifested in the way each of the divine persons is for us in the drama of salvation. In an excess of love, the Trinity has expanded its communion to include us human beings, *nos homines*.

The extent of this divine reaching out to all creation unfolds, article by article, in the creed. The Son's membership of the human race as one born of Mary, his solidarity with us in suffering the drama of the human condition, his condemnation, execution, and burial in this earth as a human failure—all are aspects of his radical being "for us." So too is his transformation in the resurrection, his sending of the Spirit, his bringing creation with him back to God in the ascension, and his role as judge of the living and the dead—but that is to anticipate what we will treat below.

That this divine "for us" has not yet been accepted into our history as the foundation of our being-for one another is brought home in the phrase "for our salvation," *propter nostram salutem*. The incarnational "for us" reaches into the depths of what we most fear—right into all we need to be saved from. Likewise, it includes the transcendent limits of what we hope for—liberation from all evil and life to the full. God's relationship to us in Christ, the divine "for us," has room for the whole of what we are and are becoming. It is the space in which the whole drama of human history is enacted. In being for us in the reality of who we are, God is not dealing with pure spirits, but with the defeats and despairs, the hopes and loves of flesh-and-blood human beings: "for our salvation." Divine love has thrown itself wholly into the complex business of making us human beings whole.

The creed implies, then, that the Son is sent to be for and with us in our common destiny—"for us" in the uniqueness of the human vocation in the midst of God's creation.

The Son is for us and with us in the burden and promise of human uniqueness. We are conscious beings embodied in this world. At the same time, we are creation-become-conscious-of-itself. The Spirit has enabled creation to "come to" itself in human minds and hearts. In what and who we are, existence breaks into a new intensity. We are the meaning-making species, unique among all the millions of species of life on this planet. In spiritual consciousness, we live not only on earth; we live within a universe. As religious beings we come to the awareness of the universe as creation. Out of the depths and direction of our being, we long to see God, the Creator of that creation in which we are immersed. We are by nature waiting on the Word to be spoken, yearning for the Spirit of final freedom to be given, longing to see the face of God. Christian faith understands human existence as being offered its crowning gift: participation in the ultimate life-form, the love-life of the Trinity itself.

The Son is for and with us, not only in the heights of human aspiration but also in the depths of our human predicament. This predicament is traditionally termed "original sin," the weight of meaninglessness and worthlessness weighing down human life in any given society or culture. In that shared bias against life to the full, manifest in our resistance to universal love and in our sheer inability to save ourselves, the Savior is "for us." However caught up in the spiral of self-destruction and in the vicious circles of our vendettas and defeats we might be, there is a way out—because love has found a way in.

Our Lord Jesus Christ is thus for and with us, both as saving us *from* alienation, despair, absurdity, and death; and as saving us *for* the fullness of life in God. Christ is the point at which creation is drawn into its divine destiny. Christ's way of being "for us" discloses both the way God is with us and the way we are with God in an ultimate way. As Athanasius so often repeats, along with the whole patristic tradition, "He became human that we might become divine" (*De Incarnatione*, 54).

Before Athanasius, another great theological thinker, Irenaeus of Lyons, pondering the whole sweep of God's dealings with creation, could exultantly conclude:

> The Lord through his passion destroyed death, brought error to an end, abolished corruption, banished ignorance, manifested life, declared truth, and bestowed incorruptibility. (*Adversus Haereses*, II.20.2)

HE CAME DOWN FROM HEAVEN

This obviously metaphorical "descent" of the Son from heaven to earth is only a problem for simple-minded literalism. It must be understood in context. Christ is the self-communication of the one "maker of heaven and earth, of all that is, seen and unseen." As present to each element of creation, God does not need to come down. All the length and breadth and height and depth of the universe is contained within the divine creative presence. Then, too, if Christ is the one through whom "all things were made," there is no depth that he does not already occupy. But this metaphor of descent is employed to evoke a sense of the original and final unity of God's creation as it is achieved in the incarnation of the Son. He is given, from the source of all, into the midst of creation to be its inner direction and meaning: "He was in the world, and the world came into being through him ... He came to what was his own" (Jn 1:10–11). Christ spans the distance between heaven imagined as the place of God and earth imagined as the place of human beings. In him heaven and earth meet. The earthly is penetrated by the mysteries of the heavenly; and heaven is the realm in which all earthly being comes home.

Further, this "coming down" symbolizes not only the unity of all creation in Christ, but also the initiative of God's freedom. God has chosen to become present personally to creation. The infinite mystery subjects itself to the limits and struggles of earthly human existence. In Christ, God is compassionately involved on the inside, in the whole groaning totality of the universe. This kind of "coming down" will take the Son to the cross, to burial among the dead, to "the descent into hell" (as the Apostles' Creed has it). Through Christ, God is present in what we imagine to be furthest removed from God—the realm of defeat, failure, hopelessness. He comes down and goes down—the self-emptying of the Son, the "condescension" of divine mercy:

> Though he was in the form of God, [he] did not regard
> equality with God as something to be exploited, but
> emptied himself, taking the form of a slave, being born
> in human likeness. And being found in human form, he
> humbled himself and became obedient to the point of
> death—even death on a cross. (Phil 2:6–8)

The Son—"Light from Light" and "true God from true God"—now lives out his relationship to the Father from within creation. Because he comes down, the Trinity is revealed as a limitless compassion enfolding that creation to itself.

While the metaphor of Christ's descent thus accentuates the unity of creation and the initiative of divine compassion, it still remains awkward to today's more evolutionary sense of reality. Classical times envisaged reality as a great ladder of being. Quite naturally, such a sense of reality suggested metaphors of ascent and descent. It imagined God above, the uppermost reality, holding the great ladder of being upright: God above, the earth below. Today with an evolutionary model of thought, given the brilliant explorations that have probed into the cosmic history of the universe as it emerges through billions of years from the Big Bang to the present moment, reality is imagined as a stupendous, ever-expanding fertile process. The accent now is less on an upward and downward vertical movement on a ladder of being and more on the horizontal, on what is coming to be, in the interconnected emergence of everything in the great universal process.

The cosmic story unfolds from an unimaginable initial explosion of energy (the Big Bang), some 10 to 15 billion years ago. Within 2 billion years, the huge clouds of the galaxies condense. Then follows the cosmic brewing of various atomic elements and the formation of the more complex compounds without which life could not emerge. In the midst of some vast inter-stellar cloud our solar system comes into being about 5 billion years ago. The earliest forms of life on earth emerge within another billion years, to develop into multicellular forms only about a billion years ago. From the early animal life of the oceans appearing half billion years later, thirty phyla survive into the present. Human life, as we might recognize it today, seems to arise approximately two million years ago—quite a latecomer in the cosmic story. But in the human mind and heart, the universe becomes conscious of itself, to awaken to itself as a divine creation, in all the splendor and variety of existing things.

Against such a background, science contemplates the great chain of being unravelling in a cosmic process of intricate and amazing interconnections. The interlinking of all reality becomes increasingly complex when, for instance, the human mind emerges as an ecstatic, self-transcending relationship to the whole. Given such a horizon, any reflective faith is inspired to a new effort of imagination. The incarnation is less a matter of the Son "coming down" than a divine act by which the Son emerges from the innermost depths of reality. The mystery latent behind and beyond the cosmic process now emerges within it. God is self-communicated in Christ as the catalyst of the final stage of what is coming to be.

In other words, God created reality as a self-transcending movement. The Spirit moves within the dynamics of the universe to enable the most primitive forms of reality to become more complex, to move beyond themselves in the direction of life; to stimulate life to leap into consciousness; and so to awaken human consciousness to intimacy with the original mystery in its faith and hope and love; finally to become familiar with its God-given meaning in the Word made flesh among us. The Word is incarnate in the living flesh of the cosmos. Life, in a new and final form, has appeared, to draw all to itself. Inextinguishable light now shines in the huge darkness of space and time; the reality of an ultimate love is enfleshed there.

12

THE MYSTERY INCARNATE

> ... by the power of the Holy Spirit,
> he became incarnate from the Virgin Mary,
> and was made man.

BY THE POWER OF THE HOLY SPIRIT

As the creed now sharpens its focus on the incarnation, faith is
once more led into a mysterious negativity. Christ is given to us by
a power not of this world: the Holy Spirit. A properly divine level
of creativity is at work before which the human mind and heart
must stand silent. When this Spirit acts, "nothing is impossible
with God" (cf. Lk 1:35–37). This "power at work within us is able
to accomplish abundantly far more than all we can ask or
imagine" (Eph 3:20): the scope of the Spirit is not enclosed within
the limits of human capacity or imagination.

The Holy Spirit breathed forth by "the Father, the Almighty"
brings into being the Christ, as the unique incarnation of the
Word. The Spirit is at the heart of God's special, supremely
personal mode of action. In the Bible's multi-faceted witness, the
Spirit is the cause of creation and life (Gen 1:2; Isa 32:15, 44:3–5;
Ps 104:30); this same Spirit gave the heroes of Israel their
liberating strength (Judg 3:10, 6:34, 11:29, 13:25, 14:6, 14:19;
1 Sam 10:6), enlightened the sages (Num 24:2; 2 Sam 23:2; Isa 9:5,
11:2), and inspired the prophets (Hos 9:7) to be oracles of God's
saving Word and to work wonders (Isa 61:1 f.). The Spirit of God

both fills the world (Wis 1:7) and works in the successive generations of God's people to prepare it for what is promised (Gal 4:29).

In the New Covenant, the power of the Spirit brings history to its peak, enabling Mary, the virgin daughter of Sion, to bring forth the Holy One. For his part, Jesus is conceived by, filled with, moved by, and anointed with this Spirit (Acts 10:38). In his Spirit-filled existence, Jesus performs his works of healing and liberation (Lk 4:14–18), and contends with the spirits of evil (Lk 11:20). In surrendering his life to God for the sake of the Kingdom, he offers himself "through the eternal Spirit" (Heb 9:14). Through the Spirit, the Father raises the Crucified One from the dead (Rom 8:11), and the Church is born (Jn 3:5; 7:37 f.). As the radiance of the Spirit streams from the face of Christ, it transforms believers from glory to glory (2 Cor 3:18), to raise us to final Spirit-filled existence (1 Cor 15:44; Rom 8:11). If Jesus is the mediator between God and humanity, the Spirit is the medium in which God's transforming action takes place.

In following the traditional sequence—Father, Son, and Spirit—the creed will explicitly turn to this Holy Spirit as "the Lord, the giver of life" in its third major article, as we shall see below. But already in the presence of the vast scope of the Spirit's action, the creed anticipates what is to come. The Spirit is the divine personal power at work in bringing about the Son's incarnation in the world. Thus the creed breaks out of any over-rigid ordering of the divine persons as Father, Son, and Spirit. By placing the Holy Spirit, in this instance, between the Father and the Son, by introducing the Spirit before the incarnation of the Son, the creed implicitly opens the way to a fresh consideration of the *filioque* controversy, as we shall see below. More generally, the fact that the creed has placed the Spirit both before and after the incarnation allows for the full narrative display of trinitarian life before it becomes crystalized in the more abstract logic of trinitarian doctrine. The Trinity is a doctrine because first of all it is a story—the narrative of how God so loved the world and acted "for us ... and our salvation." The trinitarian story is the deep structure underlying the creed's exposition.

By anticipating the Spirit's role in the incarnation, the creed is already adoring "the Lord, the giver of life" as the limitless creativity in which the almighty Father acts. Through the Spirit, God brings the whole Christ into existence: from the act of creation to the formation of Israel and the faith of Mary; from the incarnation of the Word to the resurrection of the Crucified; from the outpouring of Pentecost to the transformation of all creation in the life of the world to come. All such mysteries are phases in the revelation of the Holy Spirit.

Faith can live only in surrender to the limitless creativity of the divine power of giving and acting. Never reducible to an elemental energy within creation, the power of the Spirit subverts and judges the powers of the world. In acknowledging the Creator Spirit at work through creation, faith relativizes the power-structures constituting the so-called "real world" of any given time. In surrendering to the limitless possibilities of what God alone can do, faith expands to its proper proportions. The glory of God's gift outstrips mere human potential. Our expectations and plans can never prescribe or predict how the Spirit will act. Nature does not exhaust the possibilities of grace. The heart must always remain open to the divine surprise. Hence Paul reminds us that "we speak of these things in words not taught by human wisdom but taught by the Spirit, interpreting spiritual things to those who are spiritual" (1 Cor 2:13).

HE BECAME INCARNATE

The eternal procession of the Son within God ("begotten, not made") is the foundation of the genesis of all creation ("Through him all things were made"). But that genesis of creation in him, in all its powers of becoming more, looks to another kind of genesis: the Word becomes flesh. As the offer of a new and final becoming, the Son is now present within the process of the world's becoming. As incarnate, the Word is no longer outside or beyond, but within the actual world that is coming to be. When the Son is one of us, God is present to the world in a new way. In the Word's becoming flesh, the flesh of creation is opened to its final destiny.

The Gospels, by drawing believers into the communion

existing between the Son and the Father, promise the gift of the life-giving Spirit of their communication. Out of this fundamental experience of divine communion, the doctrine of the Trinity will eventually arise.

For the Son to be incarnate in the world means that neither the reality of God nor the reality of creation is diminished. The divine reality is revealed for what it is—Love giving itself into the limitation and darkness of creation's freedom and independence. On the other hand, the integrity of creation is respected. In the incarnation there is no fusion of the divine and the human into some hybrid existence composed of a divine and a human element, and therefore not fully either. Jesus Christ is not a mythologized centaur, as though belonging to neither the divine nor the human realm. In its classic attempt to articulate a grammar of expression designed to respect the realism of God's self-gift in Christ and the genuine humanness of Jesus, the Council of Chalcedon in 451 (seventy years after the Council of Constantinople in which the Nicene Creed was solemnly adopted) would define with great precision,

... One and the same Son, our Lord Jesus Christ,
the same perfect in divinity and perfect in humanity,
the same truly God,
and truly man composed of rational soul and body,
the same one in being with the Father as to his divinity,
and one in being with us as to his humanity,
like us in all things except sin,
begotten of the Father before the ages in his divinity,
but in these last days,
for us and our salvation,
born of the Virgin Mary, the Mother of God
    [*Theotokos*], in his humanity.

In the language of this classic doctrine, Jesus Christ, even while being one of us in a completely human way, remains throughout one with God, as the divine self-expression. The divine realm of being and relationship, and the human realm of belonging and becoming, are not to be confused. The incarnation takes place:

in two natures without confusion or change,
without division or separation,
the distinction of the natures not being abolished by the
    union,
but, on the contrary, the properties of each nature
    remaining intact,
and coming together in the one person or subject,
not by being split or divided into two persons,
but one only unique Son, God, Word, Lord Jesus Christ ...
    (Neuner & Dupuis 1983)

There is no "confusion or change." The incarnation means the dissolution neither of the divine identity of who Jesus is, nor of the human reality of his existence among us: "The distinction of the natures was never abolished by the union, but, on the contrary, the properties of each nature remained intact." Nor is there "division or separation"—as if the two realms of the divine and human had nothing to do with one another. As God's original self-expression, the Word, is freely given into that part of creation which, in its own way and on its own level, can express the divine—he becomes human. The dignity of human being consists in its capacity to so express the divine. When infinite Love seeks to express itself to creation, the human is created to receive it. We are here to receive the Gift and to glorify the Giver.

Consequently, the incarnation does not imply that the human is invaded by the divine as by some foreign subjugating power. In Christ, human existence finds its most complete meaning and far-reaching freedom. To be human is to be open to the infinite, to listen for ultimate meaning in a history of patient searching and longing, in the hope of being spoken to. Thus, in the incarnation, the impossible possibility of the human is fulfilled: ultimate meaning is received and given into what we are. The divine Word becomes human in this man, as the self-expression of the divine; and the human is most intimately united with its final goal.

In the incarnation God's intention regarding us human beings is realized. The human capacity for God is no longer a distant possibility, but something already actualized in the existence of

Jesus Christ. The presence that secretly powered all the self-transcendent becoming of the universe over its billions of years, in all the dynamics of its complex material organization, in the emergence of life, in the dawning of consciousness, in the struggle and creativity of human history, in its waiting on the mystery to reveal itself, is now disclosed when the Word becomes flesh.

Whatever the complexities of speaking of the communication between the divine and the human, faith is dealing with the "one Lord, Jesus Christ": what Jesus is in his divine identity, he is for us: he is God among us, God with us, Emmanuel. The divine and the human come "together in the one person ... not by being split or divided into two persons, but one only unique Son, God, Word, Lord Jesus Christ."

Theology may well ask what it means for a divine person to live with a human consciousness. It can explore how the Son "finds himself" in the history of a particular human freedom, just as it can wonder how the language(s) he learned and the traditions he inherited could express who he was in relation to the One he invoked as "Father." But the basic datum of faith is that he is God-with-us. In him, the divine reality is revealed and God is met and invoked. The Son's eternal relationship with the Father, in the giving and receiving of the Holy Spirit, becomes in his human existence a dialogue of prayer.

The incarnation in this way affirms both what God is and what we are: God as self-expressive Love; and human beings as "so loved" (Jn 3:16). As Christian existence unfolds "in Christ," it becomes aware that in him both the human and the divine have met, to be newly disclosed. The divine is not a threat to our humanity, but the space in which our humanity is fully realized. God is among us, not as falsifying what it means to be human, but as expressing the fullest scope and radiance of our humanity. The man Jesus radiates the light of an ultimate humanity because his is the humanity of God. The Spirit inspires faith to a realistic sense of God's love reaching into the flesh-and-blood reality of the human drama, of God with us on the inside of the human predicament: "By this you know the Spirit of God: every spirit that confesses that Jesus Christ has come in the flesh is from God" (1 Jn 4:2).

From the Virgin Mary

The Holy Spirit, though not reducible to any created power, nonetheless acts within the powers and freedom of creation: the incarnation comes about both from beyond and yet from within the realm of creation. As theology would say, precisely because the divine power so transcends the created order, it can work so immanently within it. Though the Son is incarnate by the power of the Spirit, he is still truly "born of the Virgin Mary."

Mary of Nazareth is the name of a historical person—the mother of Jesus. History has no records of her life except in the documents of faith, above all the Gospels of the New Testament.

She is eminently the women of faith. Her self-surrendering "Yes" to the design of God, her life of prayer and compassion, carry over to her presence with the disciples awaiting the outpouring of the Spirit that had so possessed her from the beginning. She is remembered in the early communion of faith as the Mother of the Lord. She stands in that early tradition as the woman living at the end of the history of her people's longing for their savior, for the Christ that would be born, and for the Spirit to be poured out on all flesh. In her, "the Virgin Daughter of Sion," all the hopes and faith of her people are condensed. Elizabeth, summing up the Old Testament praise of the faithful, proclaims, "Blessed is she who believed that there would be a fulfillment of what was spoken to her by the Lord" (Lk 1:45). While she is an end, a final point, she is also a beginning. Through her consent, in her yielding to the Spirit, the Word adored in her faith is conceived in her womb. Through her, God enters the world. She is the God-bearer, *Theotokos*. Henceforth her whole life and destiny are bound up with her Son, given over to the mystery of who he is and what he means, both then, now, and for future ages.

The Father has chosen to give what is so intimately his own, the Beloved Son, into creation—through Mary. In her consent two freedoms join: the freedom of God to give what is God's alone to give, and the human freedom of Mary, acting in the power of the Spirit, to receive it.

In hailing her as "the Blessed *Virgin*," faith is expressing two things. God's act of self-giving is not restricted or conditioned by what creation can produce in terms of human reproduction or generation. In confessing her as the "virgin" Mary, the creed invites us to adore the unique capacity of the divine freedom to bring forth the new, the culminating reality of God-with-us, the Word made flesh. The genesis of the divine Word in the human world is outside the genetic capacity of any created process. The Word is not a product of nature, but the revelation of divine freedom. When Love comes to dwell with us, it transforms all it touches.

Still, God has chosen a human cooperator: Jesus is born of the Virgin Mary. Inspired by the Spirit, her faith defines her being: she is pure receptivity to the Spirit, pure attention to the Word, pure adoration of the Father: "for the Mighty One has done great things for me" (Lk 1:49). She is defined in no other way, by no other relationship—neither by a human partner nor by social expectations. What determines her existence is solely what God can be and what God can do—who God is for her and who she is for God. She is the woman who most intimately knows that for God nothing is impossible (Lk 1:37). In her faithful existence is inscribed the conviction that the gift of God is given out of divine freedom, not as a result of human merit or ambition or evolutionary process. In her, divine freedom communicates with a created freedom. Divine Love calls for a human love to be its partner in the world's transformation.

It should be noted that the meaning of Mary's virginity implies neither a glorification nor a demeaning of human sexuality. In naming Mary as the Virgin Mother of the Lord, the creed is essentially confessing the sheer grace of God, the divine ability to bring about a new creation. Whatever intimacy and generativity there may be in human eros, such love does not simply bring God down from heaven, to make the divine either our instrument or our property. God comes because God gives. And God gives because God freely loves and chooses to do so. And in choosing to do so, God inspires a freedom in the other, the Virgin Mary, to receive and cooperate.

The Blessed Virgin is invoked only in the communion of faith. Outside of the mystery enveloping her, she cannot be known.

Consequently, her virginity has meaning only within the universe of grace. At this point, faith must learn its own reserve. There is no place for any form of theological voyeurism, in a vain effort to reduce God's "impossible ways" to the humanly familiar. It is also well to emphasize that the virginal vocation of Mary becomes apparent only in the light of the resurrection of the Son and the outpouring of the Spirit. It belongs to a new language of the world's transformation in Christ. Love has broken through as the sovereign power at work in the universe.

In that light, the faithful turn to Mary, standing with the disciples at Pentecost to recognize her unique role in the self-communication of God. In her virginity is embodied the intensity of surrender and dedication now demanded of all believers. By acknowledging her virginity, faith reaches another point of its deliberate "un-knowing" of the mystery. There, God is let free to be God; to be the impossibly gracious gift we most need, even as it remains outside our control, our comprehension, and our merits. At such a limit, the virginity of Mary is an icon of the divine, not an emblem of some body-negating asceticism.

The Spirit active in all creation and in all generations through history brings that creation and that history to a unique point of freedom in this woman. She consents on behalf of all creation to receive into itself the mystery from which all existence derives. She is the world's overture to the Word. Within the totality of the world, as a woman in the history of her people, she is named Mary, the daughter of Sion, a woman of Israel, the model of the Church: all the faithfulness of generations before her and after her, all their waiting on God and their yielding to the Spirit, are condensed in her: "Let it be with me according to your word" (Lk 1:38). She is creation's Yes to both its future and its past. Her "fiat" is the word of youthful enthusiasm and radical acceptance—in contrast to starker expressions of resignation to the divine will in the shadow of the cross.

Mary is confessed as *Theotokos*, "God-bearer," Mother of *God*. She is not the mother of Jesus' humanity merely, not the producer of a "nature," but the human mother of the person who, in his radical identity, is "God from God." The eternally begotten one is really brought forth, born into the world of creation, subjected to it. "Born of a woman" (Gal 4:4), he would know poverty, live in surrender to God, enter into the risk of living for God—and suffer the consequences. Mary's motherhood means that the divine Son is not posturing in a humanity, but is the humanization of the divine in the pain, darkness, and joy of human existence. In the womb of Mary, the world holds a divine reality within it: the Mother of Jesus is the Mother of God.

As bringing forth the Christ in the power of the Spirit, Mary can be contemplated as an icon of the Father. In the sword that pierces her heart, in the request she makes of her Son, in the silent love of her life, in her standing at the cross, she embodies the patient life-giving love of the Father. For the generations that have addressed her as Mother, she expresses the tenderness of the Father who has given what is most intimately his own for our sake. She brings forth the one whom the Father begets. She acts in the power of the Spirit with which the Father acts, to give her son for the world's salvation. Against the distortions of religious fantasy, Mary embodies a corrective to any excessive masculinization of the divine.

AND WAS MADE MAN

Here the creed comes to a reverent pause. The liturgy instructs us at this point to bow our heads (even to genuflect as at the Christmas Masses of the Latin Rite). This phrase acknowledges the holiest moment in our history. The eternal Son has become one of us, a human being with us.

"And was made man." The searching restlessness of our existence, all inarticulate longings for the original "You" felt at the heart of our being, pause at this moment of silence and fullness. "You," now, are here among us.

The incarnation is, of course, not a single moment. It unfolds in the drama of a human and, indeed, a cosmic history. The Word has entered into the complete process of human becoming, within the whole emerging event of the universe itself. He is born, grows, awakens to human consciousness, speaks human words, communicates with fellow human beings, receives into his mind and imagination the varied beauty of creation. He knows human weakness and human temptation. He is at the mercy of others for good and for ill. He suffers the price of freedom in the path he choses: he is condemned, crucified, dies, and is buried. All this is involved in the incarnation. And more: in his resurrection and ascension he becomes the promise of a new humanity in a transformed creation.

In a deep sense, his becoming man is a continuing event. It will not be complete until the love he embodies, the cause he lives for, the Spirit he breathes, finally include all who will come to call him "brother"; until all are members of his Body, until he is clothed with the whole of creation, and that creation is itself transformed.

The Son becomes man, but not in the sense that Jesus is an already existing human being somehow adopted into union with God. What and who this human being, this man, Jesus, truly is— *is* God-with-us. God is not hiding behind this human being, or somehow concealed within this human life. All that Jesus is as a human being is God in the flesh. In him, God walks among us in the garden of the new creation.

Jesus is the Word made flesh in a particular culture and within the accents of a particular language, within a lifetime in a particular history, in the limits of a particular geography. His life is a human career, lived in the light of a particular consciousness, imagination, and freedom, envisaging a particular future and remembering a particular past. He finds himself in the context of particular relationships—in communication with family, friends, and enemies, with those who call him and respond to him, with those who praise and condemn, bless and curse him.

More, he becomes human within the history of a particular faith. Israel's prayers and hopes, its law and its prophets, its promises and its God, are his own. The one whom he will address as "Father" is the God of creation, of the Exodus, of the prophets, of "the Chosen" into whose history he is born.

Christian faith is focused not primarily in a doctrine or a theory, nor in a theology or a philosophy, nor even in a creed or a holy book, nor in an idea or an ideal. It is a relationship to one who breathed the air of this planet with us, and who beyond death remains present to us—still as a human being marked with the wounds of living among us. Nourished by the flesh and blood of his living reality, believers keep finding and receiving him, to move in the energies of his Spirit in order to witness to the new realm of life he embodies. This particular man, born of Mary, is the savior of the world. What he is opens to enfold the whole of creation. And what the whole of creation is meant to be, is condensed, expressed, enacted in him. When our hearts invoke him as "You," we find God, ourselves, and all that is, re-meant and re-valued. If the creed confesses that he is God made man, then neither "God" nor "humanity" can ever mean the same again.

In this man, God has become human; and our flesh and blood and mind and imagination are united to the divine, drawn into the love-life of the Trinity itself. He is mediator, not as halfway between God and humanity, but as God among us in the flesh. A human brother is one with God in person. Theologies and theories rightly abound, since our minds must ever ask: How? Why? What is coming about in this becoming? Who is he, and how do we know him? But we end where the Gospels end. Words cannot contain the Word. For the love embodied in his presence to each of us and all creation, no human language is adequate:

> But there are also many other things that Jesus did; if
> every one of them were written down, I suppose that
> the world itself could not contain the books that would
> be written. (Jn 21:25)

Here the creed leaves us with a question: If he who is "of one Being with the Father" is now "of one being with us," what does being human now mean? Faced with this human being, with the Crucified One now risen—"Behold the man!" (cf. Jn 19:5)—much learning, and unlearning, awaits us.

13

Even unto Death

———

For our sake he was crucified under Pontius Pilate;
he suffered death and was buried.

For Our Sake

Once more the reprise, "for our sake," emphasizes that the creed
is not dealing in abstract religious information, but with God's
saving relationship to us. It is all about a gift and our experience
of such giving. The Son is here given into the depths of human
need, into the darkest of all human experiences—failure, betrayal,
condemnation, torture, execution, burial as a criminal—our
"problem of evil."

Because he suffered "for our sake," Jesus becomes *our* Lord.
What has happened in Christ means that God is identified with
our cause, saving and promoting what is *ours*, in every moment
and dimension of human existence.

Although, in terms of historical time, the crucifixion of Jesus
recedes from us in time, it is not so in terms of the active presence
of the love it reveals. The Spirit of love that led him to the cross is
the same Spirit that makes us remember, in this present moment,
the unconditional love revealed in the cross. Jesus, then and now,
is "for us," forever marked by the wounds of his passion. The
intimate presence of the Crucified and Risen One is the
atmosphere in which the Gospels were written, and which now
communicates to this later generation of believers. Because the

"We believe" of the creed is extended in history, the love at work "for our sake" is manifest in an ever expanding manner.

To be "for us" is the basic law of Jesus' life and mission. He lives and lays down his life for others, "for many" (Mark 10:45), for the world. His divine character as Son of the Father makes him uniquely "the one for others." Since his existence is intrinsically relational, the basic gesture of his being is eucharistic. His whole being is offered to nourish us, for whose sake he lived, died, and rose: "This is my body given up for you, my blood poured out: do this in memory of me."

The New Testament is constantly recalling how he was "for us." In the rich symbolism of chapter 13 of John's Gospel, the relational character of Jesus' existence is strikingly portrayed. The hour of his departing from this world and going to the Father reveals the other-ward direction of his identity—what some call his "pro-existence", his being-for-us. The Gospel expression is more simple: "Having loved his own who were in the world, he loved them to the end" (Jn 13:1 f.). The more related he was to the Father, the more intense was his self-involvement with the plight of those he loved. In the face of impending betrayal (v. 2), when knowing "that he had come from God and was going to God" (v. 3), he washes the disciples' feet (vv. 4–17). His being from-and-for-God coincides with his being for-our-sake. Paul, chiding the Philippians to "look not to your own interests, but to the interests of others" (Phil 2:4), invites them to imitate the self-giving character of Jesus: "Let the same mind be in you that was in Christ Jesus" (v. 5). The truth of his divine identity was manifest in his unreserved service of others: "though he was in the form of God ... [he] emptied himself, taking the form of a slave" (Phil 2:6–7). In an intensely personal moment, Paul can say, "I live by faith in the Son of God, who loved me and gave himself for me" (Gal 2:20).

In Christ is expressed the basic momentum of truly personal life—in the case both of God and of humanity made in God's image. In the deepest sense of the word, personal existence is interpersonal. In being for us, as pro-existent on our behalf, Jesus enacts among us the trinitarian life to which we are called.

Not only does what he enacts reveal such a form of life as a model and a promise, he nourishes us into it, as was mentioned above. We are given to eat and drink the reality of this life and to breathe its Spirit. The logic of eucharistic existence is inescapable: "Just as I have loved you, you also should love one another" (Jn 13:34).

HE WAS CRUCIFIED

When confronted by the reality of unconditional Love, the powers of evil infesting history go into a final destructive spasm. He who offered the world its true life is crucified. In the ancient world the cross was an obscene reality. It was a mode of execution reserved for slaves and subverters of the Roman empire, to deter those who were deemed to be "non-persons" because of their threat to society. It was only after crucifixion as the ultimate deterrent had been abolished by Constantine that the cross became a Christian symbol. It is difficult to capture the sense of emotional and cultural shock resulting from connecting God, Christ, or divine love to such a hideous form of death. That the divine being could reveal itself in such a way had to be experienced as religious scandal and a philosophical folly. God could not be, could not act, like *that*!

Yet precisely in that experience of shock, the utter excess of divine mercy and solidarity with the suffering was displayed. In the cross of Jesus, the excess of evil was met with that excess of love which nothing in all creation could gainsay. In the providence of love working through all events, the most potent gesture of human evil was made to dramatize the extravagance of God's unconditional love for sinful humanity: "Christ died for the ungodly ... God proves his love for us in that while we still were sinners Christ died for us" (Rom 5:6–8). The "for us" of Christ goes to an unimaginable limit, to find us at that point where our history is most against God, most closed in the vicious circle of violence, self-enclosure, and despair.

The cross of Jesus is not some capricious divine punishment or test. It is a divine gesture of unconditional love. For Jesus it is the fate that follows from his refusal to be anything but exclusively for-the-Father—and consequently "for us" in the realm of salvation. In Paul's language (1 Cor 1:20–25), Jesus crucified is a stumbling-block to those of his own people who looked for a more obviously triumphant messiah. And to the Gentile philosophers who conceived of a divine reality utterly unaffected by evil and suffering—impassable, immutable, in-human, and ultimately unconcerned—the cross was a folly of the most fundamental kind. We might add, too, that any religious linking of this criminal executed by Roman authority to the revelation of the one, true God had to be profoundly subversive of the fabric of imperial power. The "Divine Caesar" bore no resemblance to this condemned and executed criminal.

Through the culture shock that the cross occasioned, Christian faith proclaimed another kind of power at work—an infinite compassion acting only in the vulnerability and evidence of love: "God's foolishness is wiser than human wisdom, and God's weakness is stronger than human strength" (1 Cor 1:25). Every religious hope, every philosophical system, every political power had to be jolted by such a brutally "un-divine" fact: "For the message of the cross is foolishness to those who are perishing, but to us who are being saved it is the power of God" (1 Cor 1:18).

In the event of the cross the trinitarian reality of God is dramatically portrayed. The Father, "the Almighty," refuses any other presence in the world except that of his crucified Son. In his turn, the Son rejects any identity in this world save that of being totally surrendered to his Father's all-inclusive cause. The Spirit will act in no other way, will show no other power, except that self-giving love whereby the Father gives his Son and the Son surrenders all to the Father "for our sake."

UNDER PONTIUS PILATE

The real God acts in a real world populated by real people: Jesus, Mary ... and Pontius Pilate. Here the creed is not dealing with a mythological past populated by archetypal figures. The crucifixion happened in a particular place, at a particular time, under a particular provincial administration of the Roman empire: "under Pontius Pilate." This small historical expression sets the cross in the factuality of human history, geography, and political organization. It is the key to a fuller dramatic story.

One of Jesus' own disciples betrays him to the parties that for some months had been plotting his destruction. They hand him over to some Jewish leaders. From the Sanhedrin he is taken to the Roman governor. Pilate sends him to the local puppet king. Herod sends him back to Pilate, who offers him to the mercy of the mob. Betrayed by one of his own, denied by the leader of those he had chosen to walk with him, left for lost by the rest of them, libeled by false witnesses, exposed to the inflamed crowd, he is condemned by the religious and secular authorities alike. And Pilate takes the political decision that had to be made to secure the peace.

He lived and died in a real world of fear, betrayal, self-interest, and political expediency. It was not an ideal world, either then or now. The light shone, but in the shady world of distorted justice, religious intrigues, political oppression, and foreign occupation. Though he lived to draw all into a kingdom of divine mercy, he found himself at the mercy of others—of those who, through fear or greed or spite or despair, decided that none of their respective versions of the real world had any place for him.

His relationship both to God and to others for the sake of God was not a tranquil spiritual life. It unfolded in a world of politics. It had political consequences; with political implications and a political price to pay. As then, the same now … Faith is ill-advised to think it can be itself without making a political difference. If to follow him is found to demand solidarity with the defenseless and the poor, faith becomes a political option. The creed's "under Pontius Pilate" invites believers today to be ready for the inevitable political reaction to a realistic following of the Crucified. More positively, it invites Christian faith into fresh creativity in forming a new politics in a world where what he died for can mean something in the history of hope.

By so naming the particular official in that place and time of the Roman occupation of Palestine, the creed reminds us that the persons and events of its history can be historically investigated. Historical research does not replace the firmness of faith, but grounds it in the flesh and blood factuality of what really happened. Faith has room for fact. Not confined to the realm of myth or symbolism, faith expresses itself with a larger sense of reality, of how the real God acted, and continues to act, in a real world. This man, Jesus of Nazareth, born of Mary, crucified under Pontius Pilate, is a historical figure. While faith lives in his presence now, it does not do so by dis-incarnating itself from the past. The Christ is this Jesus, the man condemned and executed by Pontius Pilate. And this human being—living and dying at a particular time, in a particular place, caught up in a particular political situation—is the living Christ of our faith.

As truly a human being, the Jesus of Nazareth who met his fate "under Pontius Pilate" can be investigated by historical scholarship as it examines the documents of the past. Such an investigation can only make faith more firmly anchored in the human realities of our lives. It faces us with the particular reality of his decisions and way of life in the times and culture he inhabited, thus to inspire a more realistic faith today. In the "days of his flesh," he did not walk above the earth, but on the ground: he left footprints in the dust of Palestine and memories in the minds of friends and adversaries alike. Historical investigation cures us of that Docetism which, being so caught up in its own religious projections, can never fully accept that he is truly one of us.

HE SUFFERED DEATH

He was made man and he suffered death, the final limit of our existence. He is swallowed up into the silence, darkness, poverty, powerlessness, and separation that mark every death. And in his death there are the further intensities of suffering: agony of mind and body, betrayal, abandonment, condemnation, torture, mockery, failure, execution … He suffers death as one put to death when everything is wrapped in the greatest darkness of all, the sense of the terrifying absence of God in an impenetrably God-forsaken world.

He is neither a post-resurrection Christian nor a Jewish martyr. The manner of his death followed from the uniqueness of his mission. Crucial to his suffering was the vulnerability of being totally for God in a world where God does not seem to figure, where the "Reign of God" seems an utter unreality, where love and mercy do not seem to mean much, where God's power to save seems ineffectual, where other forces and powers are far more successful in moulding and motivating the "real world." In that sense, he died *of* God, died because he had been so much from God, for God, dedicated to his Father's will. He breathes his last, vainly invoking his God, and hangs before the world as a crucified corpse.

AND WAS BURIED

With the burial of that tortured body, the God of Jesus too is apparently buried. That kind of God has no place here. The kingdom of that kind of God is populated only by human failures, by those who refuse to adapt to the way things are and ever will be. Jesus is buried in a black hole in which faith and hope and love—all the deepest God-related aspects of our lives—are swallowed up and come to nothing.

He goes down into the world of the dead. As the Apostles' Creed so enigmatically puts it, "he descended into hell." However we imagine this state, he goes down to the point we most dread, where no life or love or divine presence seems to exist. Yet, in this dead man, divine love gives itself to the world, not only of the living, but of the dead: God is present, the Son is "for us," not only on the surface of life, but in the depths, within the whole lost past of our world.

At that point beyond any human hope, there is no automatic resurrection, no luminous conviction that death means spiritual release or personal expansion. Here death means death. In him, dead and buried, the eternity of love takes time to go down into the most dreadful dimensions of human experience. It allows for the whole of human grief when, in terms of any human imagining or communication or relationship, it is all over. Love enters into that region of the lost where the proclaimer of the new life of the Kingdom of God is now nothing but a dead body in a stranger's tomb.

Faith must wait in emptiness and grief through this day before it can be known as "Holy Saturday." We need to feel the whole deadly weight of reality pressing upon us as failure, guilt, and desolation. On that "unholy Saturday," nothing is happening; it is all over; nothing has changed. When God is obviously so powerless, all we can do is grieve and wait; and wonder if God can still act; and if so, when and how …

14

HE IS RISEN

—

On the third day he rose again
in accordance with the Scriptures …

ON THE THIRD DAY

"On the third day" marks a historical memory of three decisive
days. The Friday had ended in the shock and grief of Jesus'
execution while the Saturday dawned as a dreadful day of
emptiness. Then, on the Sunday, something happened, as
indescribable then as it is now. In the light of this eventful Sunday,
the Friday of that grief and shame would finally be called "Good,"
and the darkness of that Saturday would be called "Holy."

The reference to the three days also locates the testimony of
various witnesses of what took place. These men and women
could recall a definite time as a decisive turning point. They knew
the moment in their different ways—Mary Magdalen, "the
women," Peter, other disciples—when their sorrow turned to joy
and their world could never be the same again.

"On the third day" sounds with a further scriptural resonance.
Biblically, the phrase means "in God's good time," the moment
when God will act to reveal his glory and his power to save: "…
prepare for the third day, because on the third day the Lord will
come down upon Mount Sinai in the sight of all the people" (Ex
19:11); "On the morning of the third day there was thunder and
lightning, as well as a thick cloud on the mountain … Moses

brought the people out ... to meet God" (Ex 19:16–17). "The third day" of biblical symbolism suggests that God has time for us in a way that is beyond our capacities to make time for God. The third day dawns after the tomorrow of human calculation or prediction. God comes in God's own time, giving faith time to experience the depths of human need and to awaken in longing for what only God can do: "After two days he will revive us; on the third day he will raise us up, that we may live before him" (Hos 6:2).

And so the three holy days: the Friday of the dying, when love goes "unto the end"; the Saturday of waiting for what only such love can do; the Sunday where love is revealed in its transforming power.

HE ROSE AGAIN

In the resurrection, the love that God is, that gave what is most intimately its own into the deepest darkness of the world, is finally revealed as victorious. Already the decisive transformation has occurred. As the energy stronger than any death we know, love has had its way.

Faith in the resurrection means not only that something momentous happened as a unique divinely wrought event. There resulted a new comprehension of everything in the past and the future. The disciples now recalled what had been happening, and looked forward to what would keep on happening, with a new sense of how God is present and acting both in history and in the universe itself. The resurrection is a culminating event in the history of revelation. In its light, the whole reality of how and what and who God can be "for us ... and our salvation" was newly understood. In that awareness, the Gospels were written. They do not simply record what Jesus said and did and suffered. Nor do they merely interpret what happened. Illumined by a decisive factor missing from the ambiguous pre-resurrection world, the Gospels communicate the whole, saving truth of what had taken place. The early witnesses were so secure in their new knowledge that they were freed to admit the ignorance and puzzlement they had previously experienced. They could recall his teaching and questions, his riddles, parables, and hints—and their own resistance, confusion, and false expectations. Though they had noted with alarm his predictions of impending crisis, though they witnessed the wonder of his miracles and acts of forgiveness, felt the sheer authority of his presence and heard his promise of a new age of limitless grace, they had expected something quite different. But now they saw what it all meant, and what the whole thing was moving toward … They now had the key; and that key was an event so momentous that all their humbling remembrance of the past had to be re-shaped to tell of what was really going on. And the New Testament documents—"inspired" writings for the life of faith—were composed with an extraordinary creativity. The writers involved had to find words where no words were easily found. They had to re-read the precious writings of the past from a vantage point never accessible before. In the presence of the risen Jesus, the whole world as they had known it had been made new.

When the New Testament speaks of the resurrection, it does so only from within the reality itself. It is not talking *about* an event in a dispassionate objective manner, but passionately participating *in* and living from it. Here a number of points can be emphasized.

First of all, what was called the resurrection meant that Christ Jesus was now present in the saving totality of what and who he was. In proclaiming the Reign of God, he had indeed preached and taught and healed and acted. He had lived for the cause of his Father; and by suffering rejection, betrayal, and condemnation, he had died for it. With his resurrection, he is given back in the fullness of his reality; he is disclosed in his identity as being uniquely and wonderfully from God and of God, in all that he was and is. As Son of the Father, the Crucified and Risen One is able to be "for us," beyond the limits of time and space, in the love, power, and vitality of God: the resurrection confirms the identity and mission of Jesus. He is present as the one who saves.

As a confirming and completing event, the resurrection is the fulfillment of the incarnation. In his victory over death, the Reign of God is irreversibly made manifest. God is "with us" in a new way, and our humanity begins to live in its God-given glory. He is "here"—coming in the power of God from beyond death, greater than our guilt, despair, or limited expectations, as one affirmed by the Father, and now accessible to all in the Spirit.

Secondly, in the resurrection not only does Jesus become victoriously present to faith in all that he is—in his words and deeds, in his body and spirit, in his identity and mission; he is given back by God as a sheer gift. He is, in person, pure grace, given into the world that had rejected him. His resurrection is a gift surpassing any other kind of giving or expectation we know. Jesus is not simply resuscitated, for he has died to this life. He is not a ghost or a soul: he is present in palpable bodily objectivity. Nor was his resurrection the fulfillment of a general theory or a clearly defined hope. After all, the Sadducees did not believe in the resurrection, and the Pharisees associated such a hope only with the saints on the last day. Moreover, the prevailing currents of Greek philosophy would have found any suggestion of a new embodied existence far too physical. Besides, the disciples themselves had collapsed in disillusionment. Given such a background, the Risen One is God's surprise, outside the scope of the theologies, the philosophies, even of the prayers of the world he lived in.

If the resurrection is God's surprise, it is most so as the outpouring of limitless mercy. The Risen Jesus personifies sheer forgiveness. Love has not be turned into rejection or vendetta. It has kept on being itself to prove not only stronger than death, but more powerful than the complex of shameful evils that had destroyed him. The Crucified One is risen, not to reproach the disciples with their failures, but to draw them into the true and eternal life—the truth and endurance of which they had previously doubted. John's Gospel describes the sheer grace of Christ's risen presence, as he breathes forth the Spirit on the disciples:

> Jesus said to them again, "Peace be with you. As the
> Father has sent me, so I send you." When he had said
> this, he breathed on them and said to them, "Receive
> the Holy Spirit. If you forgive the sins of any, they are
> forgiven them; if you retain the sins of any, they are
> retained." (Jn 20:21–23)

Jesus' gift of peace and reconciliation means that the disciples, once themselves forgiven, are sent forth as the agents of divine forgiveness.

Thirdly, the resurrection is the inspiration of mission. Energized by the resurrection, faith is not distracted into an other-worldly domain, but called to witness to the deepest reality of the world as it now actually is. From the Risen One, an expanding circle of community unfolds to include all peoples, and even all creation. The disciples are sent into the world with the consciousness of belonging to a new humanity as it has been realized in Christ. Grace and forgiveness are now the key to our coexistence. Relationships based on division and recrimination are abolished. The open circle of love explodes the vicious circles of mutual victimization and aggressive self-justification. The emblematic antagonism existing between Israel as "God's Chosen People," and the rest of the nations of the world is healed at its root:

> For he is our peace; in his flesh he has made both
> groups into one and has broken down the dividing wall,
> that is, the hostility between us ... So he came and
> proclaimed peace to you who were far off and peace to
> those who were near; for through him both of us have
> access in one Spirit to the Father. (Eph 2:14, 17)

The Gospel message, then, is not primarily a new teaching but a disclosure of a new graced coexistence in the risen Lord. The Good News promises no induction into a form of esoteric enlightenment reserved for the elite. It is a *catholic* (literally, "all-embracing") communication in the service of all in Christ and Christ in all. Nor is faith intent on founding or promoting another particular kind of religion: it lives in the wonder of God's astonishing mercy, whatever one's religion, as it has been revealed in Christ Jesus.

The novelty and surprise of the resurrection is necessarily related to the reality of the empty tomb. Its discovery is fixed on "the third day," just as it contains a personal reference to "some women of our group" (Lk 24:22) who reported it. On the one hand, it never was, nor could ever be, that Christian faith could find its energy by focusing on the mere emptiness of the tomb. Indeed, in the original accounts such emptiness gave rise only to further perplexity and fear (cf. Mk 16:8; Lk 24:5, 11). There was no point in seeking the living among the dead. The joy of the disciples arose from their encounter with the crucified Lord, now living and life-giving. These early witnesses had no inclination to haunt a grave-site. They did not linger among the dead. Life now consisted in a full-bodied connection with the risen Jesus. This Jesus who had been crucified was now the form and the source of a new and ultimate vitality. In fact, the disciples' assurance of Jesus' victory over death stands in stark contrast to the original ambiguity they felt at finding his tomb empty.

Still, that emptiness did have its place in the full-bodied nature of their experience. Precisely as an index of the radical reality of the resurrection, the blank fact of the empty tomb is lifted out of its original ambiguity. The inclusion of the empty tomb in the Gospel accounts prevents our faith from remaining on an idealistic or mystical plane. To omit or downplay the testimony to the empty tomb is to find oneself veering very quickly into believing in a mere theology instead of the transforming divine happening which gives all theology a reality to think about. Incidentally, to omit the evidence of the empty tomb means bypassing the special role of women in communicating the Gospel of new life! A legend would hardly base its case on the testimony of women in a culture that scarcely accepted their credibility.

The empty tomb stands as a kind of historical marker for a transcendent mystery. It expresses a demand—set right there in the history of human defeat and failure—for faith to wake to its full realism. In a sense, the empty tomb is a negative sign: an absence pointing to a presence; an emptiness that invites to a new fullness. Faith in the resurrection is not realistically satisfied, say, by merely putting a positive construction on the continuing significance on Jesus' message. The courage of Christian conviction is based on something more real and objective. God has truly acted in raising up the Crucified in the reality of a world hitherto locked in death. In that assurance, faith comes to the tomb, not to stay there, but to break forth into a new sense of wonder: because he is risen, everything is changed; the universe is now different. To enter into this empty tomb is to be challenged to stake all on the real victory of the love. The sting of death has been drawn (Acts 2:31; 1 Cor 15:54 f.).

The empty tomb plants the seeds of wonder and questioning in the ground of history. It is profoundly disturbing for any version of a world hermetically sealed against the extravagances of love. What it stands for is too good to be true; besides, any life built up on calculation and control does not usually welcome surprise ...

Strangely, it might seem, the empty tomb, even though it is recorded in each of the four Gospels, does not draw attention to itself. Note how it is omitted from the explicit wording of the creed. For it points beyond itself. From the beginning, faith is caught up in the movement from the tomb—first discovered as a perplexing fact—to the living reality of the Risen Lord, as this was disclosed in his various appearances. But then faith returns to the tomb to recognise it as a pointer to the transformation of all creation. In the energy of that vision, faith lives out its witness in a horizon bright with the impossible possibilities of God.

What is clear is that there is no evidence of defensive embarrassment regarding the abandoned tomb. Nor, for that matter, is there any indication that either friend or foe thought that the tomb contained the remains of Jesus. The Gospel writers are quite aware of the allegation that the corpse had been stolen. That would have been a quite predictable explanation on the part of those for whom Jesus had to stay buried (Mt 28:1–15)! Still, the fact that his corpse was not left moldering in a grave is never simply a proof of the resurrection. Believers must look elsewhere: "Why do you look for the living among the dead?" (Lk 24:5). Here, too, the emptiness of the tomb underscores the advantage of Jesus' going away (Jn 16:7). Restricted by no earthly condition, held by no earthly tomb, he is present as the source of ultimate life.

IN ACCORDANCE WITH THE SCRIPTURES

The resurrection occurs as the fulfillment of the biblical witness to God's saving action. The God of all creation, the God of Israel's election and deliverance, the God who hears the cry of the poor, has acted. The whole history of the saving acts of God culminates in the decisive act of raising up the Crucified. This deeply unified sense of history flows into faith from the consciousness of the Risen One himself. As Luke's Gospel expresses it:

Then beginning with Moses and all the prophets, he
interpreted to them the things about himself in all the
scriptures. (24:27)
Then he said to them, "These are my words that I spoke
to you while I was still with you—that everything
written about me in the law of Moses, the prophets,
and the psalms must be fulfilled." Then he opened their
minds to understand the scriptures, and he said to the
them, "Thus it is written, that the Messiah is to suffer
and to rise from the dead on the third day …"
(24:44–46).

Once more the point is there to be made. Christian faith is not
dealing with a God different from the God of Israel. Both Jews
and Christians adore the one God and share the hope that such a
God will bring deliverance from all evil in the fullness of time.
The more we surrender to the demands of such adoration and
hope, the less our differences can be set in concrete. After all,
when the New Testament writers refer to "the scriptures" they
mean the Holy Books of Israel and the revelation and promise
there recorded. The different ways Jews and Christians re-read
such a past is the basis of both separation and reconciliation.
When all is said and done, both are looking for another kind of
"third day" when the light of God will shine. Till then, it is a
matter of waiting through those other days, however tragic they
may be, in patience and hope; but most of all in the spirit of a
deeper adoration of the one God of the world's salvation. For us
Christians, we can never sufficiently ponder the words of Jesus
addressed to the Samaritan woman, "… we worship what we
know, for salvation is from the Jews" (Jn 4:22). While Christian
faith clings to Christ as the decisive appearance of this salvation,
it must never forget the special election of his people, in the way
that Paul, a true son of Israel, so piercingly expresses: "If you do
boast, remember that it is not you that support the root, but the
root that supports you" (Rom 11:18).

15

The Ascension

———

... He ascended into heaven
and is seated at the right hand of the Father.

He Ascended into Heaven

Again, the play of metaphors: in the comprehensive sweep of the creed's "for our sake," he "comes down," finally to ascend, to "go up." While the limitation of spatial metaphor is clear in depicting the incarnation purely in upward and downward movements, the creed is here intending to express the whole span of God's redeeming act. In the ascension of Christ, divine love now includes all the distance between the realms of the living God and the mundane, agonizing reality of created existence. What we understand ourselves to be "from below" is joined with what God is doing "from above." The ascension, too, is "for our sake":

> But God, who is rich in mercy, out of the great love with
> which he loved us even when we were dead through our
> trespasses, made us alive together with Christ ... and
> raised us up with him and seated us with him in the
> heavenly places ... (Eph 2:4–6)

Thus, the ascension of Jesus into heaven is not simply the end of the journey for himself alone. It is of universal significance; a new beginning for all who will follow him, "so that in the ages to come [God] might show the immeasurable riches of his grace in kindness toward us in Christ Jesus" (Eph 2:7). The Exalted One now embodies the destiny to which we are called, "For we are what he has made us, created in Christ Jesus for good works, which God prepared beforehand to be our way of life" (Eph 2:10).

Ascended into heaven—into the realm of God's glory— Christ Jesus fills all time and space in a saving power encompassing all creation. No longer contained by the time and space of earthly limitation, he is present to everything and everyone in the life and intimacy of the Spirit. Though his journey from the world into God may be experienced as an absence, it is also a new presence in the sphere of faith: "it is to your advantage that I go away, for if I do not go away, the Advocate will not come to you; but if I go, I will send him to you" (Jn 16:7).

Faith does not cling to Jesus as a cult object localized at some earthly place. By letting him go into the glory of the Father, believers receive him back, in every moment and place, in the presence of the Spirit. The ascending Lord draws faith beyond the world of projections and fantasy. Faith is not meant to be always looking up into an imaginary heaven for a lost hero. It greets Jesus as the one who has come and will keep on coming from out of the luminous reality of God into the reality of this world:

> ... as they were watching, he was lifted up, and a cloud
> took him out of their sight. While he was going and
> they were gazing up toward heaven, suddenly two men
> in white robes stood by them. They said, "Men of
> Galilee, why do you stand looking up toward heaven?
> This Jesus, who has been taken up from you into
> heaven, will come in the same way as you saw him go
> into heaven." (Acts 1:9–11)

In ascending, Jesus moves beyond the restrictions and limitations that structure our present human existence. The natives of Galilee must now live as citizens of a much larger world. The whole of creation is filled with Christ's saving presence.

From the glory of heaven, the Lord fills the space left by his earthly absence. He has opened our earth to the hidden reality of heaven. In the memory of what he said and did and suffered, we have the essential icon of "our Father in heaven": "Whoever has seen me has seen the Father ... Do you not believe that I am in the Father and the Father is in me?" (Jn 14:9–10).

The ascension does imply an ending. The privileged time of the eyewitness disciples who lived their lives at the historical beginnings of Christian witness is over. Now Christ is accessible only through their word and the spiritual gift of faith: "Blessed are those who have not seen and yet have come to believe" (Jn 20:29). The new age has begun, and the ascension of Jesus Christ now points into the space God has made for the whole of human history to unfold, to work itself out in the freedom of the faith.

Therefore, the spatial significance of the metaphor of ascension—Christ going up into a cloud of glory—must not be left to the mercy of naive interpretation. For Christ, the ascension is the fulfillment of the resurrection. For believers, it means entering into the universal presence of the Lord with a new kind of freedom and consciousness: with freedom, since God is now adored only in self-surrendering faith; and with a new consciousness, since the presence of Christ Jesus is no longer contained in the time and space of earthly existence, but fills the universe with its saving power: "He who descended is the same one who ascended far above all the heavens, so that he might fill all things" (Eph 4:10).

AND IS SEATED AT THE RIGHT HAND OF THE FATHER

Jesus is not only taken into the glory of the Father, but seated "at the right hand." Once more a simple metaphor, but this time conveying the abiding and divine significance of Christ for the life of faith.

When the imagination of faith locates Jesus seated at his Father's right hand, it intends to express the fullness of his communion with the Father. The prayer of Jesus has been answered: "So now, Father, glorify me in your own presence with the glory that I had in your presence before the world existed" (Jn 17:5). In the answer to that prayer, all other prayers find their confidence and assurance. The love that has made time for the universe of creation and for the free unfolding of human history has come to a glorious consummation. It is from that high point that further gifts are given: "Very truly, I tell you, if you ask anything of the Father in my name, he will give it to you ... Ask and you will receive, so that your joy may be complete" (Jn 16:23–24).

The ascension, then, in its deepest significance, is the peak of the world's joy. One of us, this man, Jesus of Nazareth, who had gone down into the dark pit of this world's sufferings, is now with the Father. Death has not slammed shut the door behind him. It stands forever ajar—in him who is the way, the truth, and the life. The faith of ages has knocked and the door has been opened.

As the Risen Lord, he is the Son ascended to glory. His humanity, in all it shares with us, this earth, and indeed the whole of creation, has not been vaporized or annulled. Faith now beholds Christ Jesus as the full-bodied actualization both of God's deepest relationship to creation and of creation's most intimate bonding with God. Because the Son remains forever human, because the Word does not shake off the flesh he had become, creation is transfigured. The universe, and ourselves within it, have been drawn into the love-life of the Trinity. Subsumed into Jesus' journey to the Father, the world has come to its final glory. While faith and hope must be patient with God's patience and have time for the whole of God's good time, the assurance remains: he is in that *there* that every *here* of our lives longs for.

16
GLORY

He will come again in glory to judge the living and the dead …

HE WILL COME AGAIN IN GLORY

The creed now turns to the future. Both the past of Jesus Christ—his conception, birth, death, and resurrection—and his present—as seated at the Father's right hand—are moving toward a decisive fulfillment: he will come again in glory. In fact, the glory of Christ's return is the blossoming forth of the mystery already sown, and still growing, in the ground of history. Christ's coming in glory, the *parousia*, will be the final act of God's self-manifestation. After Love has shown its patience with the dark ambiguities of our history and given time to the full drama of human freedom, it will give the glory of fulfillment. The groaning of all creation in travail, our own groaning as part of it, and the Spirit's groaning supporting our hopes (Rom 8), will end in the birth of the whole Christ.

For Christ to come again in glory, therefore, does not imply a return after an indefinite absence. The incarnate Son will not make a re-entry after departing into an alien, extra-terrestrial zone. He will not re-appear where before he has simply vanished. He comes forth from the depths of God's redeemed creation where all along he had been the true life of the world. In that moment, his hitherto concealed presence will be revealed.

In hoping for his return, faith stretches forward to meet him in the final evidence of glory. His radiance will manifest the Father as the "almighty" source of all creation. In creating "all that is, seen and unseen," God created time so that all that had been destined to grow and come together and flower to freedom in Christ could reach its proper fulfillment. Finally present in full evidence, Christ the Lord will be greeted by creation as its original and ultimate wholeness: "through him all things were made."

What the creed expresses as his descent from heaven and his ascent to the divine realm will be revealed as his presence to all reality, in all time and space. The eucharist, by celebrating his real presence in the transformed "fruit of the earth and the work of human hands," will yield to the splendor of his presence transforming the whole of creation. What was before experienced as an absence will yield to a final form of presence in which there will be neither absence nor ambiguity. Our neighbor, in whom we met the Lord in the sufferings of time, will smile with his face, as all awaken to the reality of being one Body in him. The words of scripture and of the most solemn doctrines of the Church—legible or audible in our history of struggling communication only as marks on a page or sounds in the air—will pass into the pure poem of this one Word.

In short, the future glory of his presence will be less a return and more a coming forth from the depths where he dwelt concealed "for our sake." He will rise up from "the within" of redeemed creation. And all that we have worked for in love and justice and good conscience will find in him its vindication and fulfillment. In the words of the Second Vatican Council:

> For after we have obeyed the Lord, and in his Spirit
> nurtured on earth the values of human dignity,
> brotherhood and freedom, and indeed all the good
> fruits of our nature and enterprise, we will find them
> again, but freed from stain, burnished and transfigured
> … On this earth that kingdom of God is already
> present in mystery. When the Lord returns, it will be
> brought into full flower. (Gaudium et Spes, n. 39,
> Abbott edition)

The truth will out; love will remain; he will be revealed as the Yes to all God's promises and the Amen to all our prayers (2 Cor 1:20).

Yet, while the return of the Lord is a blossoming forth in the fullness of time, it is still the final act of grace. While it comes from within, it is not some kind of automatic unfolding or a human product. Only the God of glory can glorify, and will do so in a final act of freedom. Jesus' return in glory will be a grace completing the gifts already given. It will occur as a fulfillment in the time and in the manner proper to the impossible possibilities of the Creator and Redeemer of the world.

Faith must move forward in the presence of God's saving love revealed in Christ. The apostle urges us to stand firm. There is a truth to be lived and a fulfillment to be hoped for. While Christians must bear the burden of living and dying in a particular time of history and within the limits and possibilities of a given culture, faith must not lose its nerve. He will come. The apostle summons believers in every age to the courage demanded of them:

> In the presence of God and of Christ Jesus, who is to
> judge the living and the dead, and in view of his
> appearing and his kingdom, I solemnly urge you:
> proclaim the message; be persistent whether the time is
> favorable or unfavorable ... (2 Tim 4:1 f.)

To Judge

Christ Jesus alone is judge. Our responsibility as believers is to pass no final judgment. Faith must always defer to the time and measure of his judgment. To us is given the task of proclaiming his Gospel in patience and forgiveness, in giving and receiving, in dialogue among ourselves and with those who do not believe, and in holding the grace we have received as meant for all: "Do not judge, and you will not be judged ... Forgive, and you will be forgiven; give, and it will be given to you ..." (Lk 6:37–38). In deferring to his judgment, we believers must wait in a happy relativity as regards our judgments of others. We cannot pass absolute judgement, for we find among us neither the Kingdom of God on earth, nor an empire of evil within history. In leaving final judgment to him, we are left to make our own patient, ironic journey through time, waiting on a revelation of truth that can occur only at the end. Indeed, the irony inherent in our human condition dissuades us, not only from judging others, but from any self-justification:

> It is the Lord who judges me. Therefore do not
> pronounce judgment before the time, before the Lord
> comes, who will bring to light the things now hidden in
> darkness and will disclose the purposes of the heart.
> Then each one will receive commendation from God.
> (1 Cor 4:4–5)

And yet to believe in Christ as judge is not to anticipate some new judgment to be passed on the world. That judgment has already been made. In the Crucified and Risen One, love has not been turned into vengeance. It has kept on being love, to be expressed in Jesus' prayer for mercy: "Father, forgive them; for they do not know what they are doing" (Lk 23:34). The definitive character of the final judgment enacted in Christ is strongly expressed in John's Gospel:

> Indeed, God did not send the Son into the world to
> condemn the world, but in order that the world might
> be saved through him ... those who do what is true
> come to the light, so that it may be clearly seen that
> their deeds have been done in God. (Jn 3:17, 21)

While faith has to allow for the possibilities of created freedom to reject Christ, we still live in a universe of grace. God is not constrained by unredeemed categories of worldly justice in which the penalty must fit the crime. The saving character of divine judgment is already revealed and enacted in Christ. This kind of justice belongs to the fabric of the new creation—a universe of grace excluding no one. Whatever the dreadful possibilities of human freedom—known principally in our own selves—to reject the grace that is offered, the world, as a whole, has been fundamentally saved. God's saving intention will not be defeated: God *so* loved the world. However powerful the resistance to grace might be in ourselves or others, we are never entitled to lose hope in what God can do—and has already done. An ultimate judgment has been made; and "nothing in all creation" is able to thwart or withstand the impossible possibilities of God's love. While the community of faith celebrates the holiness of many of its members, it has never dared, for fear of denying the Gospel itself, to declare that any human being is beyond the reach of divine mercy.

It is not given, then, to human history to make ultimate judgments—save, of course, that there is one who judges, and that he has died for us. Faith looks to a judgment beyond our history, and keeps its peace, finally to leave all judgment to its Lord: "It is God who justifies. Who is to condemn? It is Christ Jesus, who died, yes, who was raised, who is at the right hand of God, who indeed intercedes for us" (Rom 8:33–34). Whatever our burdens in time, the responsibility of making an ultimate judgment is not one of them.

The creed's affirmation of a final divine judgment is, in effect, an act of hope. Faith looks to a moment of truth when all that is loveless and destructive in our experience of ourselves and our world will be revealed for what it is. God's love will come into its own. What we most treasure is not indefinitely at the mercy of what we most fear. Judgment, then, in its deepest Christian meaning is not an object of dread, but an inspiration to eager desire and prayer: "*Marana tha*! Our Lord, come!" (1 Cor 16:22); "Amen. Come, Lord Jesus!" (Rev 22:20). Fear, then, is not the best preparation for the judgment that awaits us all, "the living and the dead":

> God is love, and those who abide in love abide in God,
> and God abides in them. Love has been perfected among
> us in this: that we may have boldness on the day of
> judgment, because as he is, so are we in this world. There
> is no fear in love, but perfect love casts out fear; for fear
> has to do with punishment, and whoever fears has not
> reached perfection in love. We love because he first loved
> us. (1 Jn 4:16–19)

THE LIVING AND THE DEAD

Such a judgment comes to the living and the dead. It is worth noting that however much Christian traditions differ regarding the fate of the dead, any notion of post-mortem purification must be thought of as being effected by love and for the sake of love. In dying into God, the dead come to that moment of perfect love that casts out fear. Their existence becomes pure desire for God.

Relying on a divine judgment, faith keeps trying to find its most realistic and hopeful expression. There is no need to deny that even the best among us go to God marked by the tensions, imperfection, and unfinished business of the human condition. But to meet this judge is to encounter the ultimate love that can transform and purify. Those who have gone before us, and we who will follow after, all alike can be healed and made whole. Even as we pray that the dead may rest in peace and that eternal light will shine upon them, we realize that light eternal is searching out all darkness, to vanquish all fear of total surrender to the living God. But that light is the purifying, all-transforming flame of Christ's Spirit. In the presence of the Lord, love cannot remain imperfect; and to him who first loved us our prayers commend all who have died.

And for us, the living, true hope for this final judgment shows itself in a refusal to lose our Christian nerve. Awaiting that judgment and longing for it, faith clothes itself with the patience of God. It stands self-possessed in the midst of the scandals and ambiguities of existence in this unfinished world, where the human conversation is never complete, and time has still to run its predestined course.

17

GABRIEL'S PROMISE

—

... and his kingdom will have no end.

In this phrase, the creed incorporates into its own confession the words the angel Gabriel addressed to Mary (Lk 1:33). What God will do through Jesus Christ is not preliminary to something else. The reign of Christ will have no end; God's irreversible, climactic act has occurred. Because, through the incarnation, God will remain eternally involved in the human, our humanity has a lasting place in God. In Christ, the definitive self-communication of God to creation has taken place. While the climactic significance of such a gift slowly dawns on human consciousness, while there will be different contexts in which the gift can be understood more deeply and broadly, the reality is, once and for all, present, actual, universally inclusive: "Jesus Christ is the same yesterday and today and forever" (Heb 13:8).

In his conviction that all reality is subject to the realm of Christ, Paul defiantly asks, "Who will separate us from the love of Christ?" (Rom 8:35). He goes on to affirm, "... we are more than conquerors through him who loved us" (Rom 8:37). In that assurance, Paul is certain that nothing in life or death, nothing in the already known or still hidden dimensions of the universe itself, nothing in the past or the future, "will be able to separate us from the love of God in Christ Jesus our Lord" (Rom 8:39). Christ remains, embodying God's enduring act of self-giving love.

The realm of Christ's Lordship is one of ongoing communication. Believers—like Mary, who "treasured all these words and pondered them in her heart" (Lk 2:19)—respond by contemplating the full measure of God's gifts. Present to the praying heart is the Spirit, given as an intimate gift: "the Advocate, the Holy Spirit, whom the Father will send in my name, will teach you everything, and remind you of all that I have said to you" (Jn 14:26).

It is likewise the realm of God-given peace: "my peace I give to you. I do not give to you as the world gives" (Jn 14:27). The peace of Christ's kingdom is not a pact or treaty—not a negotiated peace. It is rather the sheer gift of the one over whom "the ruler of this world" has no power (Jn 14:30). A new realm of existence has been opened up, in which "no one will take your joy from you" (Jn 16:22). Even if this still means for us a time of waiting and praying, we have the Lord's assurance that, in his name, our prayers will be answered: "I will do whatever you ask in my name, so that the Father may be glorified in the Son. If in my name you ask me for anything, I will do it" (Jn 14:13–14).

Further, the peace and joy pertaining to the realm of Christ flow from the "life to the full" (cf. Jn 10:10) that Jesus came to give. He is, in person, the fountain of eternal life: "whoever believes in me will never be thirsty" (Jn 6:35). His kingdom abounds in a vitality beyond the destructive powers that now threaten our existence: "This is indeed the will of my Father, that all who see the Son and believe in him may have eternal life; and I will raise them up on the last day" (Jn 6:40).

The Lordship and kingdom of Christ do not mean, however, that Christ has ceased to surrender all that he is to the Father. His filial relationship is brought to its fulfillment. It expands to include all creation, so that "in him" all creation is gathered to its fullness (Eph 1:10). Those who accept him become God's children, to glorify the wonders of grace (Eph 1:6,14). As the Father glorifies the Son, the Son eternally glorifies the Father. Reflecting on the realization of Christ's reign, Paul writes, "When all things are subjected to him, then the Son himself will also be subjected to the one who put all things in subjection under him, so that God may be all in all" (1 Cor 15:28).

The endless kingdom of Christ's Lordship remains as a judgment on all earthly kingdoms. The life of the world to come is realized, not in the subjection of others, but in self-giving love. His lordship is not one of domination, but of loving service.

The Crucified One is risen to subvert the self-enclosed arrogance of all earthly pretensions. While the politics of our earthly city wax and wane in all the calculations of human selfishness, while all the ambiguities of worldly ambition await their final judgment, "his kingdom will have no end." In its vulnerability to the brute powers of this world, whatever the projections and victimization inherent in any culture, faith continues to express its simple prayer: "Jesus, remember me when you come into your kingdom" (Lk 23:42).

18

THE LIFE-GIVING SPIRIT

> We believe in the Holy Spirit, the Lord, the giver of life,
> who proceeds from the Father (and the Son).
> With the Father and the Son he is worshiped and glorified.
> He has spoken through the Prophets.

In the third major article, the creed now focuses explicitly on the Holy Spirit. The Spirit has already been mentioned in connection with the incarnation: "by the power of the Holy Spirit he became incarnate from the Virgin Mary, and was made man." That prior reference serves as a reminder that there is no moment of salvation, either in history or in the heart of believers, apart from the Spirit's involvement. Indeed, only under the influence of the Spirit can the Church now formulate its belief in the Spirit as an article of faith expressed here in the creed.

WE BELIEVE IN

This is to say that the Spirit is both an object of our adoration and the one who inspires us to adore in the first place. To speak technically, the Spirit, by being present in the subjectivity of faith, enables faith to reach its proper objectivity, and so to affirm the various articles of faith found in the creed.

By naming the Spirit, the creed once again leads us to a point of darkness—to knowing by way of negation. Our ordinary forms of knowing have now to yield to a mode of knowledge that only the Spirit can give:

these things God has revealed to us through the Spirit; for the Spirit searches everything, even the depths of God ... Now we have received not the spirit of the world, but the Spirit that is from God, so that we may understand the gifts bestowed on us by God. And we speak of these things in words not taught by human wisdom but taught by the Spirit, interpreting spiritual things to those who are spiritual. (1 Cor 2:10–13)

As we emphasized before, to believe in the Father Almighty is to adore God's love as the original and all-inclusive reality. Believing in the Son is adoring this love as a divine self-giving in the incarnation. Believing in the cross is adoring such love as unconditional in its mercy. Believing in the resurrection appreciates such unconditional love as irreversibly victorious, as truly God's act. Consequently, to believe in the Spirit is to adore this love as communicating itself in our lives through the course of history. In the Spirit, love keeps on being love, to bring all the good that God has done in Christ into this present moment.

Such an emphasis can be related to the *epiclesis* of the eucharistic liturgy. There can be no genuine thanksgiving (*eucharistia*), no fruitful communion with Christ in his life, death, and resurrection (*anamnesis*), unless the Spirit is invoked upon us (*epiclesis*). The invocation "Come, Holy Spirit!" is implicit in the whole life of faith and in the meaning of every creed. The invocation of the Spirit fittingly precedes the agenda of every Christian gathering and activity.

THE HOLY SPIRIT

The original "we" of faith now re-asserts itself as a communion "in [the unity of] the Holy Spirit." The one love in which the Father and the Son are united as a divine *We* reaches beyond itself to include the *we* of believers in its embrace. As the last breath of the Crucified (Jn 19:30) and the first breath of the Risen Lord (Jn 20:22), the Spirit is Christ's gift of the innermost principle of the love-life he embodies.

Trinitarian love has enfolded us into its own life. It remains ever *beyond* us as Father, before our beginnings and at the end. It is ever *with* us in the Son as the Word made flesh. It is ever *within* and *between* us in the Spirit. For the Holy Spirit is the limitless, creative field of love in which God and creation can communicate in the Breath of ultimate life. A divine ecstasy enters into our existence as the energy of self-giving love. In that ecstatic existence, the young see visions and the old dream dreams (Acts 2:17), and the Church is invigorated with a variety of Spirit-ual gifts (1 Cor 12:4–11): "To each is given the manifestation of the Spirit for the common good" (v. 7).

THE LORD

The Breath of Life dwells in us as Lord and God, not as an impersonal force, but as a divine *You*. Just as the Son is "of one Being with the Father," so the Spirit is of one being with the Father and the Son (Council of Constantinople, 381 CE). In the traditional order of doctrinal expression, the Spirit is the third divine person to be named. However, in terms of our experience the Spirit is the first, as the one in whom we recognize the Son and have access to the Father. The more we go out of ourselves in love, and leave behind the deadly isolation of "the heart of stone" for the vitality of the "heart of flesh," the more we share in the Spirit of God's own loving. In that Spirit, faith comes to recognize the truth of Christ and to enjoy intimacy with the Father.

THE GIVER OF LIFE

The Spirit vivifies. The Giver of Life moves within and among us in the power and energy of "life to the full." As divine Giver and Gift, the Spirit dwells in believers to open their existence to a new realm of relationships. Through that indwelling, our human selves are "christened" by being conformed to the loving existence of the crucified and risen Lord.

In every moment of creation, the Spirit has labored to bring forth life, culminating in the presence among us of "The Life" who is our Way and our Truth. This divine Breath of true life is stronger than any death-dealing power. It animates the whole of groaning creation that it might bring forth the whole Christ in the full dimensions of "the life of the world to come." The one who brought about the victory of love in the life and death of Jesus is at work within us:

> If the Spirit of him who raised Jesus from the dead
> dwells in you, he who raised Christ from the dead will
> give life to your mortal bodies also through his Spirit
> that dwells in you. (Rom 8:11)

The whole groaning totality of creation is animated by this Holy Breath, to open our lives to the fullness of life:

> For the creation waits with eager longing for the
> revealing of the children of God ... We know that the
> whole creation has been groaning in labor pains until
> now; and not only the creation, but we ourselves, who
> have the first fruits of the Spirit, groan inwardly while
> we wait for adoption, the redemption of our bodies ...
> Likewise the Spirit helps us in our weakness; for we do
> not know how to pray as we ought, but that very Spirit
> intercedes for us with sighs too deep for words.
> (Rom 8:19, 22–23, 26)

Through the gift of the Spirit, the energies of self-giving love invigorate the life of hope; "and hope does not disappoint us, because God's love has been poured into our hearts through the Holy Spirit that has been given to us" (Rom 5:5).

The Spirit's vivifying presence offers intimacy and freedom with God. Liberated to be "free and easy" with God, familiarly invoked as "Abba", we can lovingly relate to "our Father," and leave behind the idol fabricated by fearful projections. Interiorly possessed and illumined by the Spirit, each believer is enfolded into Christ's filial existence:

> For all who are led by the Spirit of God are children of
> God. For you did not receive a spirit of slavery to fall
> back into fear, but you have received a spirit of

adoption. When we cry, "Abba! Father!" it is that very
Spirit bearing witness with our spirit that we are
children of God ... (Rom 8:14–16)

Into a world of destructive obsessions, of unholy spirits
infesting human life and culture, the life-giving Spirit comes as
Holy. The dynamics of unholy possession are fueled by the
human capacity to foreclose on the whole promise of life in order
to make oneself the center of the universe, and to live in a spurious
infinity of security and control. Such is the experience of the
diabolic—literally, of being torn apart, *distracted* at the center of
our being. When our existence is so torn and distracted, we begin
to fabricate idols by projecting onto possessions, power, pleasure,
security, race, nation, or class some kind of absolute importance.
However naive or sophisticated such projections might be, they
each end in a form of self-destruction. An individual or even a
whole culture eventually sacrifices its own humanity to an all-
demanding idol. We can lose our souls as our selfhood is numbed
in its primary relationships to God, to society, and to the rest of
creation. With the idol on the outside and demons on the inside,
human consciousness has no room to expand into the universe of
grace and love and mercy. Victimization, prejudice, envy, and
greed pervade the unholy region of life closed to the holiness of
the Spirit.

In contrast, the Holy Spirit inspires the works of
reconciliation, hope, and healing. God's Spirit opens a space for a
healthy proportion, right relationships, and creative freedom: "the
fruit of the Spirit is love, joy, peace, patience, kindness, generosity,
faithfulness, gentleness, and self-control. There is no law against
such things" (Gal 5:22–23).

The holiness of the divine Spirit manifests itself in the great
values—the truly non-renewable resources—without which the
progress of any community would be impossible. Such a holiness
is both healing and whole-making, to bring peace where before
there was anger, conflict, and violence. It inspires patience and
forgiveness where before there was resentment, vindictiveness,
isolation. Self-absorption and self-indulgence are replaced by self-
sacrificing, other-regarding love. The "Lord, the giver of life" is

the inexhaustible Gift of forgiveness and new beginnings.

WHO PROCEEDS FROM THE FATHER

The Holy Spirit comes from God, not as a created energy or as a generalized creative force pervading creation, but as *God*. Like the Son, the Spirit is "God from God." Originating in the Father, the Spirit receives and communicates all that God is. Breathed forth from the divine realm, the Spirit comes always as an excess, a surprise, a gift—beyond any finite anticipation or creaturely need. By adoring the Spirit, faith affirms the limitless originality of God.

Because the Spirit comes forth from the divine depths, it is the field of life and love in which all becoming occurs. In the Spirit, the Word is eternally conceived; creation happens; the Word is made flesh; and the whole of creation moves towards its fulfillment.

In the trinitarian structure of the creed, the Father of love is adored in a twofold originality. The divine Source is self-expressive in the Son. All that God is, can be, and, in fact, will be, is uttered in the divine Word. Then, in the other depth of originality, the Father is self-communicative in the Spirit. The Holy Spirit comes forth from the Source as love for all that God is, can be, and will be for all creation. The Spirit is God's ecstatic self-giving to the other, both eternally and in time. The Father is, then, self-expressive in the Word, and self-giving in the Spirit.

Theology has long struggled with the terms in which to distinguish the Son as "God from God," and the Holy Spirit as "proceeding from the Father." How is each "God from God" in a distinctive manner?

There is value, of course, in sticking close to liturgical and biblical usage by exploiting the metaphorical sense of classic prepositional expressions. As faith participates in the trinitarian life, God is ever *beyond* us as Father, ever *with* us as Son, and ever *within* us as Spirit. More subtly still, our salvation is a communication *from* God (the Father), *of* God (the Son), and *as* God (the Holy Spirit).

The limitation inherent in such cryptic expressions is their tendency to congeal as spatial metaphors, so to block a deeper appreciation of the trinitarian mystery. Such expressions may say more about the limited scope of our knowledge of God than about the divine reality itself. An essential task for theology remains in trying to relate the more or less spontaneous language of faith to a deeper notion of what God really is. If the holy mystery gives itself as grace for human existence, what kind of self does God have to give?

Though theology can be so often more full of itself than of God, there is room for reverent exploration. In this regard, one of the most enduring analogies employed by theologians through the centuries is what is commonly called "the psychological image." The basic human psychology of being conscious of ourselves by knowing and loving has often been explored as a way of throwing some light on how and why God is trinitarian life. It suggests that the Father is God knowing himself in the Word, and loving this self-expression in the Spirit. Thus, God is self-known in the Word (including all that God is and can be and will be "for us ... and our salvation") and self-possessed in the Spirit in the sheer joy of communication. Thus, the Word/Son is the unbounded expression of the divine identity and meaning, and the Spirit is the ecstasy of joy and love that follows. In such a scheme, the Spirit comes from the Father through the Son, who, in receiving all that God is, breathes the Spirit with the Father (*filioque*).

But such an analogical scheme has met with objections, above all from the great Greek theological traditions of the East. Hence, a remark is necessary on "and the Son."

AND THE SON

The Western form of the creed confesses that the Spirit issues forth from the Father "and the Son." The *filioque* was commonly inserted in the creed from the sixth century, not to be seriously contested until some 200 years later. One of the reasons for the addition (apart from biblical passages such as Jn 15:26) was that Western theology generally felt, along with many of the Greek Fathers (cf. the Councils of Reunion), that it was necessary to add "and the Son" for fear of presenting the Son as less than the Father. If the Father communicates his whole divinity to the Son, then the power to breathe the Holy Spirit must be implied in that communication. Then, too, if the Spirit is to be distinct from the

Son, that distinction must be based on the relationships of origin. The Son cannot be distinct from the Spirit except by being one with the Father in breathing forth the Spirit. Hence the Spirit is the love that comes forth from both, to make the Spirit uniquely the Spirit of unity and peace.

Still, the Eastern Christian tradition remains definitely uneasy about such a view. Apart from the historical fact that the *filioque* was unilaterally inserted into the common creed by Rome, the Greek understanding of the Spirit finds the *filioque* formula tending to downplay the "originality" of the Spirit in Christian experience. The whole of Christian imagination tends to be fixated in the incarnation alone, and, as a result, in a given ecclesiastical order—"the institution," in modern parlance. The Spirit looks like a divine afterglow once the issues of salvation and revelation are settled. The Spirit, in all the originality of the divine gift, tends to be forgotten.

Various Church councils attempted a number of formulae of reconciliation. They saw the necessity of recognising different formulations of trinitarian doctrine as both legitimate and complementary. If you followed the Latins, you had the logical meaning, but might miss the mystery. If you followed the Greeks, you adored the mystery, but lost something of the logical meaning. Ecumenical discussions go on. Ultimately, the only resolution is to refocus all our theological efforts on the reality of God as love; and more deeply, *in* that reality of divine love— through prayer, reconciliation, and forgiveness, and an adoring trust in the Spirit.

Here, we might note one kind of insight that may prove successful in resolving some of the issues. If God *is* love, the divine being-in-love can be explored in the more profound form of the psychological image so dear to the Latin tradition. The traditional form goes something like this: we cannot love what we do not know. The more you know, the more you love the object known. Hence, in God, divine love associated with the procession of the Spirit flows from the conception of the divine Word/Son. The Spirit comes after and depends on the Father *and the Son/Word*.

But from another point of view, the more you love, the more you know. This is uniquely the case on the personal plane of knowledge. So, within the divine consciousness, analogically speaking, one may think of the Spirit as God's infinite power of loving. An ecstasy of love comes forth from the Father in which he knows and utters his divine meaning and identity in the Word. The Spirit, to this degree, both precedes and proceeds from the Son. The Spirit is the divine power of love in which the Father communicates himself in the Son, and in which the Son surrenders all to the Father. Hence, new kinds of reconciling formulae might be explored, to break open all the images of temporal sequence in which the Spirit always comes last.

A less rigid pattern, open to the play of our full experience of God as Trinity, has a certain biblical and doctrinal plausibility. For example, we read in scripture that the Spirit brings forth, guides, anoints, and witnesses to Christ, the Word Incarnate. Then, too, we confess in the creed itself, "by the power of the Holy Spirit, he became incarnate from the Virgin Mary, and was made man." In both cases, the implication is that the Father generates the Son in the power of the Holy Spirit.

True, only the dialogue conducted in faith and love can ever resolve this difficult and perplexing matter. A great grief occurs in Christian history when differing doctrines on the Holy Spirit have occasioned disunity. That is the most extreme kind of theological irony. It seems desirable, then, if this creed is to have an ecumenical future, to return to the original formulation—only, of course, if all parties concerned adore the Spirit with greater realism and generosity. In all our theological explorations, we are left with the sober reminder that the Spirit is, first of all, a gift to be lived, rather than a truth to be too rigidly clarified—a divine presence before being a human formula.

With the Father and the Son, He Is Worshiped and Glorified

The object of Christian worship is the divine community of Father, Son, and Spirit. God is not solitary, but adored as a love-life of giving and receiving. If the divine community is one of boundless self-giving love, we most glorify God in receiving that love and living it.

Worshiped and glorified with the Father and the Son, the Spirit is acknowledged as the living space of divine communion, one in whom the Father and Son surrender to each other in mutual love and delight. The Spirit is thus given as the divine impulse toward self-effacing service of the other: the Spirit of unity, love, peace, and generosity. However, the Spirit does not suppress personal distinction, either in God or in the community of faith itself. The Spirit is a personal field of unity-in-distinction, in which to be personal is to be from and for the other in love. Selfhood, in God and in the world of creation, is relational. When the creed adores the Spirit within the life of God, it is correcting any tendency to think of the Father and Son as locked in a self-enclosed, almost symbiotic unity. The Spirit is the personal realm of freedom, creativity, and self-surrendering love—allowing for genuine otherness, both within God and in the world of creation.

While the worship and glory we now offer to God the Trinity recognizes the infinite difference between the Creator and the creature, such praise flows from a certain "inside knowledge" of the divine life. The divine three have drawn us in faith and love into their own vitality. In other words, while we adore the three divine persons, while we can sing, "Glory be to the Father and to the Son and to the Holy Spirit," there is a more intimate formula: "Glory *to* the Father *through* the Son *in* the Holy Spirit." Faith does not behold God from the outside; it lives the divine life from within.

Finally, our glorification of the Holy Spirit shares in the way the Father and the Son glorify the Spirit of their unity. As the Father glorifies the Son in the resurrection, the Son glorifies the Father by offering to him the whole of creation. But both Father and Son now glorify the Spirit: "When the Advocate comes, whom I will send to you from the Father, ... he will testify on my behalf" (Jn 15:26). Jesus goes on to say, "it is to your advantage that I go away, for if I do not go away, the Advocate will not come to you" (Jn 16:7). Faith must make room for the originality of the coming of the Spirit: "when the Spirit of truth comes, he will guide you into all truth" (Jn 16:13). It is the Father's will to be worshiped "in spirit and truth" (Jn 4:24). Both the Father and the Son are now present in the world in no way other than through this Holy Spirit.

As they glorify their Spirit, the Spirit glorifies them: in the Spirit the Father is worshiped and the Son is glorified: "He will glorify me, because he will take what is mine and declare it to you" (Jn 16:14). As the Spirit dwells in believers, a life of self-surrendering love is present in the world.

He Has Spoken through the Prophets

Jesus presents himself at the beginning of his ministry as one inspired by the Spirit of the great prophets of Israel. He quotes from Isaiah: "The Spirit of the Lord is upon me, because he has anointed me to bring good news to the poor" (Lk 4:18; cf. Isa 61:1).

In the Spirit by whom Jesus was conceived, possessed, guided, and finally glorified, the Old and New Testaments are joined. The Holy Bible has come to be recognized as the one book of the Church's inspired scriptures, the one "en-Spirited" book of faith and revelation—itself a gift of the Holy Spirit to believers. Israel and the Church are thus scripturally and "Spirit-ually" related, in the one progressive movement of the Spirit's action.

Here, the manner in which the Church depends on the Spirit indwelling the great prophets of Israel is beautifully expressed in the First Letter of Peter:

> Concerning this salvation, the prophets who prophesied
> of the grace that was to be yours made careful search
> and inquiry, inquiring about the person or time that the
> Spirit of Christ within them indicated when it testified
> in advance to the sufferings destined for Christ and the
> subsequent glory. It was revealed to them that they were
> serving not themselves but you, in regard to the things
> that have now been announced to you through those
> who brought you good news by the Holy Spirit sent
> from heaven—things into which angels long to look!
> (1:10–12)

The same divine Spirit who prepared the world for Christ now possesses him and offers him to the world as its savior. As inspiring a prophetic voice through all the generations of faith, the one Spirit brings out the meaning of God's Word in history. Each generation of believers is refreshed by the Spirit in its perceptions of how God is present and acting.

Speaking through the prophets, the Spirit is the advocate of the radically *new*. The life-giving Spirit works to overcome the historical inertia that tries to secure control of the Word by privileging the past as a paradigmatic golden age. All efforts to reduce what is to come to a repetition of what has been are contested by the prophetic Spirit. It breaks the binding power of the past and impels the believer into the possibilities of the future. It does not allow any return to an untroubled existence. It caused the prophets of Israel to serve "not themselves but you" (1 Pet 1:12). It guides Peter to the house of the pagan Cornelius (Acts 11). It surprises the early community with the unsettling gift of the former persecutor, Paul (Acts 9:13 f.). In John's Gospel, the Advocate is the advantage that comes with the departure of the earthly Jesus (Jn 16:7). It leads to a prophetic knowledge of things that before could not be borne (Jn 16:12 f.). The Spirit works to open religious imagination to the radically, the unimaginably, new.

More particularly, the influence of the Spirit prevents the creed from being merely a list of articles of faith in verbal form. The Spirit's presence is life-giving, prompting traditional formulae into an excess of meaning, inspiring faith to be a continuing adventure into "the boundless riches of Christ" (Eph 3:8).

19
THE CHURCH

We believe in one holy catholic and apostolic Church.

Underlying the structure of the creed is the story of the God's self-giving love. The Church is the historical telling point for the continuance and realization of such a story. In the Church, "the seen and unseen" aspects of God's creation, the incarnation of the Word, and the gift of the Spirit come together in the flesh and blood reality of human beings witnessing to their faith.

The original love of the Father, which unreservedly gave itself in the crucified and risen Son, to now be communicated in the Spirit, is humanly materialized in the body of believers, the Church. The community of faith draws its unity from the love-life of the Trinity itself. And its mission, inspired by the generosity of such love, consists in going beyond itself to evangelize the nations, thus to be an instrument of the realization of God's universal reign. In its way, the Church is that part of the world wakened to the glory of Christ's saving grace.

WE BELIEVE IN
The *We* of the Church exists as an open circle. It is peopled by "those who have been made one by the unity of the Father, Son, and Spirit" (St Cyprian). This *We* can never be closed in on itself; for it lives within the all-inclusive range of both the incarnation and the outpouring of the Spirit—so that God might be "all in all." This *We*, if it is to be faithful to the divine will, must keep expanding through the course of history to include generations yet to be born.

Belief *in* the Church, as the creed articulates it, presupposes a life of faith lived *within* the Church. In the womb of "Holy Mother Church," the Christian community is brought forth to faith and formed in Christ. So, the Church is the matrix in which each believer and every generation is nourished with the reality of Christ and enriched with the gift of the Spirit. The Church illuminates the life of faith through her sacred scriptures, in the celebration of the sacraments, through the preaching and prayer of her liturgy, through the learning experiences expressed in her doctrines, in the authority of her teaching and discernment, and in the witnessing of her doctors, martyrs, confessors, founders, and reformers.

ONE

The Church's oneness derives from the unity of the trinitarian God. It is called to stand in history as a sign and agent of this unity-in-love. In this regard, the fundamental dynamic of Christian community can be described in terms of unification. It is centripetal: the Church must become one in seeking to live from its center, Christ, and so overcome its own divisions. It is centrifugal, too, in that the unity of the Church is continuously extended outward, to invite all the nations and peoples of the world into the unity of the Holy Spirit. Here the Church embodies Christ's prayer for unity in a twofold manner: the Church exists as one because that prayer has been answered. On the other hand, believers must keep on praying and working that the prayer of Jesus will be answered in all its fullness: "Holy Father, protect them in your name that you have given me, so that they may be one, as we are one" (Jn 17:11). This prayer of the Lord allows for history, by envisaging the successive ages of faith:

> I ask not only on behalf of these, but also on behalf of
> those who will believe in me through their word, that
> they may all be one. As you, Father, are in me and I am
> in you, may they also be one in us, so that the world
> may believe that you have sent me. (Jn 17:20–22)

This sense of the one unifying mystery of love pervades every aspect of ecclesial consciousness. Our organic unity with Christ, our sharing in a common Spirit, the trinitarian name in which we are baptized, our common vocation and hope, our participation in the *all* of God's creation that Paul here refers to—each is a facet of the one, ultimate, inclusive grace of God:

> There is one body and one Spirit, just as you were called
> to the one hope of your calling, one Lord, one faith,
> one baptism, one God and Father of all, who is above
> all and through all and in all. (Eph 4:4–6)

At this juncture in the creed, the word "one" must signal a serious statement of ecumenical commitment. The unity that the Church embodies and believes, flowing as it does from the heart of trinitarian love, inspires a unifying activity. How this further unity will be achieved and when it will be brought about, are questions finally and only answered in the future to which the Spirit leads. But there is no ambiguity attached to the imperatives of unity. Reconciliation, dialogue, shared prayer, and collaborative action are inescapable. Unless the unity of the Church is a living, unifying force, it becomes an ideology of exclusion, promising not oneness in Christ, but conflict and decomposition.

As a shared confession of faith, the creed itself is an instrument of unity. It is, literally, "binding," for it brings the various traditions of Christian faith together—close enough, at any rate, to face the differences that exist. The ample space of its meaning does not demand an inert, undifferentiated uniformity, but allows for a differentiated, organic unity.

Holy

Within, and despite, the obvious limitations of the observable Christian community, the creed expresses belief in the Church as holy. Here it is a matter of adoring, in the humility and hope of Christian realism, the Holy Spirit given to and working within the Church. For the Church is fundamentally holy only because God is holy. At the depths of its life, the Church inhales and breathes forth the Holy Breath of the Father and the Son. Such holiness does not fail: it is the inexhaustible source of the Church's grace.

In this regard, the holiness of the Church is never primarily the holiness consisting of the sum total of holy people, even of the saints in its midst. There is an unfailing principle of holiness given, present, and preceding any human response. When the Church expresses faith in her own holiness, such a confession is not an act of self-congratulation on attaining some level of spiritual, ethical, or mystical excellence. It is simply the humble confession of the gift that has been made, and keeps on being made, whatever the vicissitudes and fragility of our history. Receptive to the gracious holiness of God, the Church lives her life by "abounding in thanksgiving" (Col 2:7)—*eucharistia*. Secure in the conviction that her holiness is a pure gift, the Church—in all her members—is freed to confess her sinfulness, so to feel the summons to the ever more radical demands of conversion to "the grace of the Lord Jesus Christ, the love of God, and the communion of the Holy Spirit" (2 Cor 13:13).

To this degree, the God-given holiness of the Church is accessible only to faith. It is not a holiness somehow contained by the religious institution, nor a quality of psychological or cultural accomplishment. It is a gift that keeps on being unreservedly offered. Christ is risen and the Spirit has been given.

Belief in the one *holy* Church is an especially contentious issue today. Never before has the vast historical reality of Christianity been studied in all the light and darkness of its different periods. The results tempt many to disillusionment in the face of the human imperfection that is all too visible. The historical weight of the Church seems too heavy a burden for faith to bear. We are tempted to disencumber our personal faith of such an incubus of scandal, conflict, and confusion; to stand back from everything that is commonly termed "the institutional Church." Hence the familiar refrain, "Jesus, Yes! The Church, No!"

At such times we must ask ourselves whether we have become all too Docetic in our appreciation, not only of the genuine humanity of Jesus, but also of the historical humanity of the Church, and even of the human reality of ourselves. To prefer immediate union with Christ against any mediation on the part of a sinful Church might indeed express a profound and genuine sense of faith. Still, there is room for second thoughts. After all, it is only in the Church, through the sorry reality of very human Christian believers, that we have come to know Christ, to celebrate his presence, to eat and drink his reality, to receive his Spirit, and to hear his word in the inspired scriptures. It is possible to be so caught up in our own kinds of mean little excommunication—occasioned though they be by scandal or impatience for something better—that we miss the reality of the Church's holiness. Are we looking at the whole reality of the Church? Or are we, in a harsh, unforgiving way, censoriously fixated in some distorted fragment or other—as it appears in a particular time or place or person? Are we perhaps even trying to find an excuse for not being involved in the flesh-and-blood history of faith, with all its demands, risks, and ambiguities—to hide conveniently behind our own projections of unlivable excellence? Indeed, is our sense of scandal all too convenient? More seriously still, are we simply inventing a private sanctity based on self-justification, apart from the corporate, pilgrim existence of the Church? A conventional religiosity comfortably living *off* the Church is eventually faced with the demand to live *for* it.

The creed's belief in the "holy Church" at the very least presents the possibility that the grace of God is far more humanly incarnate in our midst than our precious, irritated moralism can perceive. As the old scholastic adage had it, "Whatever is received, is received after the manner of the receiver" (*quidquid recipitur, recipitur per modum recipientis*). Has a prim, bloodlessly exalted spirituality closed our eyes to real holiness? Will we ever know what we do not truly love?

Such a question makes the necessity of genuine Christian witness stand out even more. There are always in our midst those who have so received the mystery of holiness into their lives that they challenge the jaded routines and timid compromises of Christian "business as usual" to show a far more imaginative generosity. They are, of course, the saints and martyrs, the confessors and mystics, the religious founders and reformers, the pastors and prophets. Above all, they are the millions of good people, across the generations, for whom there is no special name. Without resentment or disgust, they live a depth of holiness often unappreciated by the scandalized, the disaffected—and the threatened. Once a sense of companionship with such as these is lost, once a common love is no longer shared, once the solidarity in faith and hope shrinks into a self-absorbed "spiritual experience," the true holiness of the Church disappears from view. In the meantime, the Church is there, populated with real human beings, sinners and saints—clothed with ambiguities yet confessing its sins, and still offering us all, in life and in death, the fullness of Christ.

Practically speaking, belief in the holiness of the Church means a call to conversion. Through the Church, the infinite gift of love is still offering itself, inviting our participation, provoking a deeper response. At every point in the Church's history, a limitless mercy is available, inspiring a fresh beginning. Even the most wholehearted love of God can discover new depths and a broader scope. Even the most generous service is humbled before the work still to be done. And however rich our understanding of the faith, the truth of Christ keeps expanding—as we pass over into the lives of others in dialogue and hold ourselves open to those further reaches of truth that genuine science or scholarship or art might offer. The reality of the Church's holiness is accessible only to those prepared to be fully converted.

CATHOLIC

"Catholic" derives from the Greek adjective *katholikos*, meaning "all-inclusive," and the adverb *kat'holou*, "on the whole," "open to the whole." It contrasts with the sectarian and exclusive, *haeresis*, "heresy," holding to the part without a saving sense of proportion.

In this regard, "Catholicism" is an unfortunate word, appearing in Christian history barely one hundred and fifty years ago. It tempts to an unhealthy abstraction. Traditionally theology was content to speak of the *fides catholica* or the *ecclesia catholica*—the Catholic faith or the Church Catholic. While "catholicity" denoted a quality essential to the historical community of Christian believers, "Catholicism," like all "-ism" words, tends to connote the ideology of a closed system. The implication of such an abstraction is that members of the churches in communion with Rome were not truly catholic, but "catholicists"—the proponents or victims of a narrow, ideological religious system. The recent history of the Catholic Church might be best understood as a movement of conversion, away from a "catholicist" exclusivism to a living catholicity of dialogue and communion. The movement toward a reconciling, dialogical manner of being the Church poses the question more urgently: What does authentic catholicity mean for the Church? What does it imply, and what does it demand?

The *catholic* implication—being open to all peoples and cultures and epochs, and to all the modes of experiencing the reality of God and the world associated with such an embrace—must mean, first of all, that the Church shares in the catholicity of trinitarian love. This reality of love is originally manifested by the one God, the maker of "all that is"; by the Father who gives what is most intimate to himself for the world's salvation: "For God so loved the *world* that he gave his only Son" (Jn 3:16). By receiving such a gift, the catholicity of the Church expands to a universe of connections centered in him through whom *all* things were made. Attuned to the life-giving Spirit who has spoken through the prophets, in whose power Jesus is born of the Virgin Mary and raised from the dead, and who is poured out on all the earth, catholicity is a consciousness of the holy wholeness of God's action in history.

Marked by such catholicity, the Church is called to live its universal mission through time, through the succession of generations, in all the variety of the world's cultures and in the provocative diversity of her own traditions. Historically, "the Catholic Church" is a title claimed by Christian communities in communion with the Bishop of Rome as holder of the Petrine office—before, and then in spite of, the schisms between East and West, the Protestant Reformation, and the great variety of traditions and churches that resulted. Yet, despite these divisions, a new age of ecumenism is now occurring, and every Christian community now has its own distinctive responsibility to maintain a more dynamic catholicity. As with its unity and holiness, the

Church can never rest content with its catholicity at any stage. Authentic catholicity of faith is always expanding. This open movement expresses itself in a reconciling and inclusive outreach, operative in all the traditions, in all the variety of rites and local cultures making up the Church.

Speaking as a "Roman Catholic," might I suggest a few examples of a more differentiated catholicity. While the nomenclature of current ecumenical dialogue has prescribed the designation "Roman Catholic," and I am a member of a church in communion with the Bishop of Rome, this must not obscure the fact that I am a member of a church in a particular diocese (the local church), in Australia (a particular culture), of the Latin rite (one of many), in communion with the Bishop of Rome (but not myself a Roman!), and called, at every level of such an identity, to the wider ecumenism of faith and love and Christian dialogue. If before "all roads led to Rome," now a traveling pope kisses the ground of every country he visits—a symbolic gesture for all his fellow Catholics.

Secondly, Catholics of the North (Europe and North America) are now faced with a huge demographic shift in Church membership toward the Southern regions of the globe: that is where 70 per cent of Catholics now live. This new situation in Africa, Asia, Oceania, and South America contrasts in many ways with that of the North. The populations are much younger and, in some cases (Asia, Aboriginal Australia), the cultures are much older than those of Europe. Certainly, as in India and Africa, they are more religious compared to the secularism of the North. Politically speaking, these Southern regions are postcolonial and, as a consequence, embroiled in the dramas of self-determination. Apart from being racially non-white (a factor contributing to the dramatic otherness of the emerging Church), these regions are economically poorer and structurally disadvantaged in the transnational organization of the global economy.

Along with the Church's recognition of the need for a larger catholicity in terms of culture, demography, and economic justice, there is a further imperative: the catholicity of human relationships—individual, social, political. The patriarchal, monarchical, feudal, masculine modes of relationships structuring so much of the Church's history must now be extended into the sexually inclusive, democratic, and interactive mode of the present. A catholicity from above is meeting with the new opportunities of a catholicity from below.

But to return to the general point. Catholicity is now experienced less as an attainment and more as an imperative to inclusiveness. Each local church community avoids isolation and eccentricity only through communion with the ecclesial wholeness of grace. On the other hand, the transcultural, international, global, and universal extent of the Church is realized only when it includes the culture, vocation, gifts, and needs of each individual community. A vast ecology of catholicity marks the present situation of the Church. For the whole Church, present in each individual community and in each local church, extends the living catholicity of the Church universal.

An even larger sense of universality is now crying out for consideration. The essential catholicity of the Church is intrinsically diminished if its faith and hope does not embrace the wonder of the universe itself. Here the question posed by Simone Weil is piercing: "How can Christianity call itself Catholic if the universe is left out?" The time of the Church is a microsecond at the end of billions of years of cosmic history. Catholicity demands that faith remember such a past, to adore the creative providence that has brought us to this point, and now takes us beyond it. If "through him all things were made," such a belief must leap to a new intensity of catholicity, and open out to a more reverent dialogue with the scientific exploration of the cosmos. For the catholicity of faith can be enlarged to wonderful new dimensions as created intelligence explores the complexity and immensity of the universe.

APOSTOLIC

In its "apostolic" character, the Church participates in the outgoing scope of God's love in Christ. As the Greek root suggests, to be an apostle is to be given a mission, to be "sent" as the bearer of good tidings. As sent by the Father, the Son is the "apostle" *par excellence*. Those who follow him enter into his life of mission; he commissions the Church to carry on, and to carry out, what was begun in him. In his prayer to the Father, Jesus prays: "As you have sent me into the world, so I have sent them into the world" (Jn 17:18). The "sending" goes on. It reaches into history from beyond history to involve us now in the mission of Christ and his Spirit. The sweep of God's saving love, as it connects the Church with its apostolic past, now sends believers into times and situations just as alien and threatening as anything the apostles before us had to face.

In confessing the apostolic movement of the Church, the creed celebrates our continuity with the founding witnesses of the past. Because they witnessed in their lives, and often in their deaths, to the truth of Christ, we rejoice in the Gospel today and face our apostolic responsibilities in the present. The Church is turned outward to a world searching for hope. Those sitting in the shadow of death where the light does not yet shine may well stop any or all of us with the questions: Where are you, where is this Church, as we strain to hear any words of light and life? Why has the Good News been so long coming to us? As we hesitate before the enormousness of the task and the prospect of a future for which there are so few signposts, the creed is here a statement of hope. Though we are sent out to take our place in the apostolic mission of the Church, the Lord is with us: "Go therefore and make disciples of all nations ... And remember, I am with you always, to the end of the age" (Mt 28:19–20).

Under such a summons, Christians today can profitably recall the varieties of apostolic witness recorded in their past. There is Mary, in the virginal totality of her faith, who surrenders herself to the incarnate mystery of her Son. There are the Johannine communities that found their center in a great affirmation, "God is love," and came to the practical realization that such love had to be lived if God was to be known. For his part, Paul is the living witness to the capacities of divine grace to convert and transform us in heart and mind to life in Christ. Then the apostle Peter, the leader of the twelve, was sent to confirm the faith of his brothers and sisters by so forming the Church that it could preserve the integrity of faith in the midst of an ambiguous world: "... you are Peter, and on this rock I will build my church, and the gates of Hades will not prevail against it" (Mt 16:18). Each of these kinds of apostolic witness continues into the present, to inspire believers to put a whole life into the cause of Christ and his Gospel.

Drawing on such a living communion of witness, the Church is still sent into "the whole world," in the different epochs and cultures of its history. Sent in this way and into such a world, the Church can never be a tranquil sect living outside of time or disengaged from the drama of history. As apostolic, the Church can never rest where it is; it is always being sent out and on, into places it may well fear to go. But the insistent universality of God's grace provokes it in every age to a more courageous, inventive apostolic witness. In such energies, the Gospel is proclaimed within the inconclusive unfolding of human history; and those who receive it with purity of heart wash the feet of the powerless and the dispossessed.

Hence, in owning this kind of apostolic faith, believers celebrate the universality of Christ's mission; and they share in the patience of God who alone has time for all, over all epochs and in all cultures—until that prayer is answered, "That they may be one."

20

BAPTIZED IN THE NAME

We acknowledge one baptism for the forgiveness of sins.

WE ACKNOWLEDGE ONE BAPTISM

The Spirit acts in the one, holy, catholic, and apostolic Church. In its turn, the Church acts by baptizing. The command of Christ continues to resonate in her life: "Go therefore and make disciples of all nations, baptizing them in the name of the Father and of the Son and of the Holy Spirit" (Mt 28:19). In its active belief in one baptism, the Church is one; it incorporates new members into the one Body of Christ. The Church is holy, for it is acting out of the fullness of its original holiness, the trinitarian life itself. It is catholic, as it welcomes believers from all times and cultures into a holy communion. Finally, in its baptismal activity, the Church is apostolic, obeying the command of Jesus to build up the community of disciples in every age: "Go therefore and make disciples ... baptizing them ... "

As Mary became the mother of the Lord in the power of the Holy Spirit, so now the Lord and Giver of Life works within the Church, to make her "Mother Church," bringing forth new life in the waters of her womb.

The sacramental water of this one baptism—poured by the one, holy, catholic, and apostolic Church—symbolizes the unfailing stream of the divine love-life flowing from its trinitarian source. To be baptized, then, is to be initiated into the deepest life of the Church, to breathe the Breath of holiness itself. The baptized become living temples of the Spirit, members of Christ, sons and daughters of the Father.

By celebrating this sacrament, the Church experiences the gift of new life. Those who are baptized are drawn into the great act of transformation that has occurred in the death and resurrection of Christ. The dynamics of a new order of existence are symbolized in the sacramental waters as immersion, washing, and re-invigoration. The believer goes down into his death, to be cleansed of the stains of an old and doomed existence, and to be made new in the life of the Risen One:

> Do you not know that all of us who have been baptized
> into Christ Jesus were baptized into his death?
> Therefore we have been buried with him by baptism
> into death, so that, just as Christ was raised from the
> dead by the glory of the Father, so we too might walk in
> newness of life. (Rom 6:3–4)

Baptism, then, enacts a radical transformation of our existence. By drawing us into the community of living faith, this sacrament symbolizes the whole new sense of reality expressed in the articles of this baptismal creed. Being a "visible sign of invisible grace," baptism celebrates a new identity in God, and leads to a new form of belonging to one another, beyond the borders of nation and culture. A transformed existence implies a new way of acting—the love and the hope of "walking in newness of life," in our journey through time. As transformed, the believer is indeed "born from above ... of water and Spirit" (Jn 3:3, 5).

To repeat: the "We believe" of faith lives from both the We of the Trinity itself, and from the We of those incorporated into the Body of Christ. The history of believers through successive generations is a continuous re-generation in the death and resurrection of Christ. The Lord and Giver of Life is the source of the true life that keeps on being life, life to the full, through the whole course of history, until the life of the world to come.

The creed's confession of one baptism implies an acknowledgment of the significance of past generations of faith, as well as of the uniqueness of each believer in the present. The baptized of the past and those of the present are united in the call to live for and, indeed, to die into the future, that the Body of Christ will grow to its full proportions in "the life of the world to come." The inexhaustible originality of the Spirit is ever bringing forth the new.

In this way, baptism is an entry into the "We" of a new creation—creation healed, transformed, made into a sacrament of the God's presence and life: "… if anyone is in Christ, there is a new creation: everything old has passed away; see, everything has become new!" (2 Cor 5:17–18). Whether the eyes of faith open slowly or suddenly, a new and wonderful universe dawns to this new vision of "all in Christ."

Faith must assume that the Spirit is at work beyond the reach of the Church. Since the Giver of Life is at work in all lives, and the Church baptizes those called to explicit faith in Christ, we can cherish the hope that there is a hidden baptism occurring throughout the world, which only the Spirit can bring about. Ancient traditions speak of a "baptism of desire" accessible to all people of good will, and "the baptism of blood" realized in those who give their lives in the cause of Christ, however implicitly they know it. Offered to the deepest desire of every life is a grace that knows no earthly limits, which has worked, and will work, in areas beyond the Church's scope. In acknowledging such possibilities, believers are often humbled by the great hope and selfless love of those who are not Christians. We must envisage unknown numbers of others with whom we are spiritually united, who have been drawn into the death and resurrection of the Lord in ways beyond human calculation. Though there are always limits to what the Church can do, there need be no limit to our hope in what the Spirit can bring about. A hope without limit in a grace without limit keeps the mission of the Church alive, as Christians work to communicate the riches of Christ within the opportunities and limitations of every age. What cannot be done must be left to God. What God wants of us is known in the Church through the command of Christ to preach and to baptize. The further reaches of this saving will are disclosed only to a hope that need set no limits to the "impossibilities" of what God alone can do. The prayer of the Church, as it surrenders to the universal saving will of God, is always outstripping our powers to baptize and achieve a visible unity. The counsel of Paul, the apostle to the nations, makes this point in a powerful way:

> First of all, then, I urge that supplications, prayers,
> intercessions, and thanksgivings be made for everyone,
> for kings and all who are in high positions, so that we
> may lead a quiet and peaceable life in all godliness and
> dignity. This is right and is acceptable in the sight of
> God our Savior, who desires everyone to be saved and to
> come to the knowledge of the truth. For there is one
> God; there is also one mediator between God and
> humankind, Christ Jesus, himself human, who gave
> himself a ransom for all—this was attested at the right
> time. For this I was appointed a herald and an apostle
> … , a teacher of the Gentiles in faith and truth.
> (1 Tim 2:1–7)

FOR THE FORGIVENESS OF SINS

In associating baptism with the forgiveness of sins, the creed points to a radical liberation in the life of the baptized. Our existence is no longer defined by guilt; the story of life is not reduced to the sum total of our failures. There is always a new beginning being offered in the healing grace of the Lord. The words of the Risen One, addressed to disciples who knew their own depths of guilt in abandoning him, are instructive for all ages: "Peace be with you. As the Father has sent me, so I send you … Receive the Holy Spirit. If you forgive the sins of any, they are forgiven" (Jn 20:21–23). The Spirit, not our sins, is now the defining principle of our lives.

In the one movement of healing grace, forgiveness received must show itself in forgiveness given. Any calculation of the worth of others, any judgment on their moral status, any concern for their relationship to God, must yield to another sense of proportion. At the beginning of the call to repentance is an unconditional love. Any summons to repentance that omits or distorts the assurance of boundless mercy is in deepest contradiction to what has been revealed in Christ.

It follows that any Christian judgment on the world or this present age cannot rightly be one of recrimination or dour moralizing. Our relative judgments must, of course, be made; but not so as to operate outside the domain of a boundless mercy. The ever greater mystery is always mercy, not evil. It is the inspiration of all the works of forgiveness, reconciliation, and reaching out to the other—especially when that other is so easily defined as a sinner. In the universe of grace, there is no meritocracy. To exist at God's mercy is to be left with nothing but God. In the nakedness of this kind of utter surrender to the God of mercy, there is nothing to cling to—not even our sinfulness—as an excuse for holding back. In the parables of the universe of grace, a prodigal son is met and welcomed home by a delighted father; the good shepherd carries back the sheep that had strayed; and the widow celebrates the recovery of her lost coin.

In its belief in "the forgiveness of sins," the creed frees Christian existence from the dead weight of the past and all the hopeless burden of self-justification and recrimination. The original sin of victimizing the other and being victimized in return, of asserting our own righteousness at the expense of others and excluding them as impure from our supposedly holy company, is replaced by this original grace of forgiveness in the Spirit.

In contrast to a worldly identity structured on the exclusion of others, Christian selfhood is reborn in Christ to breathe another Spirit. It issues forth in the petition, "Father, forgive us our trespasses as we forgive those who trespass against us." As a result, our identity as Christians breaks out of the vicious circle of self-justifying judgment. It leaves behind the idolatrous forms of defensive, individualistic self-assertion for the sake of a humble entry into the merciful universe of "*Our* Father." There grace reigns, Christ has died and risen for our sake, and all holiness comes from the Spirit.

21

THE LIFE OF HOPE AND THE HOPE OF LIFE

We look for the resurrection of the dead,
and the life of the [age] world to come. Amen.

WE LOOK FOR THE RESURRECTION OF THE DEAD
In these concluding phrases, the "We" of the creed envisions an ultimate communion in life beyond death. In the light of Christ's resurrection and in the energy of his life-giving Spirit, the Church looks forward to its fulfillment "in the life of the world to come." Faith becomes unbounded hope in its conviction that "neither death, nor life, nor angels, nor rulers, nor things present, nor things to come ... , nor anything else in all creation, will be able to separate us from the love of God in Christ Jesus our Lord" (Rom 8:38–39). Our Lord Jesus Christ is "the resurrection and the life" (Jn 11:25); and the unending life he promises consists in union with him, and the One who sent him into the world for our salvation: "And this is eternal life, that they may know you, the only true God, and Jesus Christ whom you have sent" (Jn 17:3).

Eternal life, as a living communion with the Father and the Son, has already begun. Whatever our questions on how the Spirit will bring faith to its fulfillment, the life of the world to come is a life that has already come into this world (Jn 1:4). However changed the conditions of our risen existence might be, the resurrection of the dead is not strictly an "afterlife" as far as our basic relationship to God is concerned. The creed envisages the fullness of life as the glory and completion of what has already begun within us. Whatever images Christians might use to speak of the final fulfillment of life in God, however hidden such life might be in the rough fabric of our present existence, it cannot be thought of except as the blossoming forth of the relationships we already have with the God who has first loved us (1 Jn 4:10). John's letter catches the sense of present actuality, of hiddenness, and of promised fulfillment:

> Beloved, we are God's children now; what we will be has
> not yet been revealed. What we do know is this: when
> he is revealed, we will be like him, for we will see him as
> he is. (1 Jn 3:2)

Faith thus passes over into hope. It anticipates completion in the ultimate possession of the peace that the world cannot give; in the final delight of that joy that no one can take from us; in the full evidence of the truth that sets us free; in the plenitude of the abundant life Jesus came to give; in being possessed by the love that nothing in all can creation can resist. The dark night of faith looks to the dawn of its final day.

In all the images and anticipations of the end, the paschal mystery of the death and resurrection of Jesus remains the basic parable. United with the Lord in his death, faith yields to the Spirit in a new creation:

> If the Spirit of him who raised Jesus from the dead
> dwells in you, he who raised Christ from the dead will
> give life to your mortal bodies also through his Spirit
> that dwells in you. (Rom 8:11)

In their present reality, as in their anticipation of the fulfillment of life in God, believers already stand in communion with those who have gone before them. Though the dead are absent from this present life, they have died into life's ultimate mystery, the true future of the world, "the life of the world to come." In the vitality of that holy communion—"the communion of saints"—the presence of the martyrs is of supreme importance. Witnessing to Christ unto death, these who were violently removed from the world are given back to us in the communion of faith. They are present to us in the Spirit, as witnesses to a love that is stronger than any death we know. In them is already realized the life that is hiddenly and courageously growing, despite the ambiguities and violence of our present history.

In confessing the resurrection of the dead, the creed emphasizes the reality of those who have died in faith. They are already incorporated in the risen Christ and, indeed, in the transformed universe embodied in him. The dead are not disincarnate souls. They are newly embodied, we might say, in the Body of the Risen One. As the bread and wine of the eucharist become, through the power of the Spirit, our "real food and real drink" (cf. Jn 6:55), so our embodied existence is being brought to its fullest reality in a transformed world.

In looking "for the resurrection of the dead," the creed lays the foundation of a sense of compassionate solidarity with the dead. The sober side of Christian realism is a humble admission that not all of us (any of us?) go into the presence of the Lord as wholly integrated into Christ and completely possessed by his Spirit. The perfect love that can cast out all fear is not yet our common possession. In all the variety of prayers for the dead, Christian tradition has expressed its total trust in the purifying power of Christ's love, along with a sense of solidarity with the human reality of the individuals we are. Death must contain a moment of judgment, purification, and final grace. In that moment of truth, we hitherto fragmented beings are given the integrity of perfect freedom in which to make an act of total, unrestricted surrender to Christ. The doubts, hesitations, compromises, and distractions of our multilayered existence yield to existence as a "living flame of love" (St John of the Cross). In this way, the Holy Spirit is "the fire of purgatory," purging our existence for union with the all-holy mystery of God.

Praying for the dead is, then, an expression of believing in the "resurrection of the dead." In Christ, we stand with them, in the reality of who they and who we are, and of what must occur for all of us—to be given over to the purifying and healing grace of God. The prayer of the Church is inspired by the all-merciful Spirit, to make each of us part of the final healing and liberation of all who have gone before us. Such is the solidarity of compassion, of the way we belong together in forgiveness, reconciliation, and intercession. As our prayers and love accompany the dead in their final transformation, death does not break our communion. Love reaches into death's darkness to become a prayer that they be given eternal rest and that perpetual light might shine upon them. The Church enfolds each of the dying in the ancient prayer:

> Go forth, Christian soul, from this world, in the name
> of God the Almighty, who created you; in the name of
> Jesus Christ, Son of the living God, who suffered for
> you; in the name of the Holy Spirit, who was poured
> out upon you; go forth, faithful Christian. May you live
> in peace this day; may your home be with God in Sion,
> with Mary the Virgin Mother of God, with Joseph, and
> all the angels and saints.

AND THE LIFE OF THE [AGE] WORLD TO COME

The final word of faith is an affirmation of life. Whatever the mortality and decay that characterize this present world and the fragility and incompleteness of our lives within it, the world to come is one of life to the full. While "no eye has seen, nor ear heard, nor the human heart conceived, what God has prepared for those who love him" (1 Cor 2:9), the God of our faith is the very life of the new creation. For the destiny of creation is to be enfolded into the love-life of the Trinity itself. Faith hopes for the fullness of such a holy communion: "The glory that you have given me I have given them, so that they may be one, as we are one, I in them and you in me, that they may become completely one" (Jn 17:22–23).

The life to come, as we have already stressed, is already present in the reality of love enacted among us: "We know that we have passed from death to life because we love one another" (1 Jn 3:14).

The love that has grown within us, the love that never ends (1 Cor 13:8), leads to the light, the vision of God face to face. The "beatific vision," as it has been traditionally termed, means that we shall meet God in full evidence, to receive into our hearts and minds the glory of the Light. But as the climax of our union with God, the vision of God "face to face" is also the culmination of God's communication to creation. In those who see God, the original, self-giving, unconditional love of God for creation is achieved—God "all in all" (1 Cor 15:28). In the words of St Irenaeus, "if the glory of God is the fully living human being, the fullness of that life is the vision of God" (*Gloria dei vivens homo; vita autem hominis est visio dei*). The redeemed will

> ... feast on the abundance of your [God's] house,
> and you give them drink from the river of your delights.
> For with you is the fountain of life;
> in your light we see light. (Ps 36:8–9)

AMEN

A great Amen, after the two hundred or so words used by the creed to describe the various articles of faith, concludes in a final simplicity and commitment. The experiment of faith involves those who believe in a life of decision and affirmation. The decision of faith is always in the making, given the inevitable ambiguities inherent in our existence in this world. It is formed in the face of false gods offering lesser versions of life. But faith is also an affirmation—of life, of love, of hope; of meaning over absurdity; of mercy, too, despite the harm we cause and suffer. When faith demands such decision and affirmation, its last word has to be "Amen," emblematic of that purity of heart for which all believers struggle.

This "Amen" expresses a commitment to make sense of it all, in humility, patience, and trust—trust in the Spirit and trust in the collaboration of fellow believers within the continuing tradition of Christian belief. The Amen of faith is not one of passivity, of drifting along on a religious tradition. There is no room for inertly living *off* the life of faith. Believers must live *for* it. Believing always means self-involvement, with the Amen of each of us living and dying into the ever expanding community of the faithful from generation to generation.

And yet this firmness and acceptance is not some self-willed choice. It is a response to the gift that has been given. From beginning to end, Christ is "the Alpha and the Omega" (Rev 22:13), the first and the last letter of the alphabet of Christian existence. In him we find the "Yes" to all God's promises and the "Amen" to all our praying and believing (2 Cor 1:20; cf. Rev 3:14). The Amen, as the concluding endorsement of the creed, draws its strength from the power of the trinitarian love that has brought us together as the "We" who believe, even as we look to full and final evidence:

> ... it is God who establishes us with you in Christ and
> has anointed us, by putting his seal on us and giving us
> his Spirit in our hearts as a first installment.
> (2 Cor 1:21–22)

Thus, the meaning of Christ as the "Amen, the faithful and true witness, the origin of God's creation" (Rev 3:14), is unfolded in the various articles of faith, to be decisively underscored in the Amen of our common faith, the signature-word of the true believer.

To the source of all love in the Father, Amen!
To the self-gift of love in the Son, Amen!
To the boundless mercy of love in the cross, Amen!
To the victory of love in the resurrection, Amen!
To the Spirit as the communication of that love through all
    time and space, Amen!
To the celebration of such love in the Church, Amen!
To the final glory of this love in the life of the world to come,
    Amen!

FOR FURTHER READING

As a beautifully presented and illustrated resource for teachers, I strongly recommend Jean-Noël Bezancon, Philippe Ferlay & Jean-Marie Onfray, *How to Understand the Creed*, John Bowden (trans.), SCM, London, 1987.

To understand why and how the creed has emerged as such an important ecumenical focus today, essential references are the three World Council of Churches publications under the editorship of Hans-Georg Link: *Apostolic Faith Today: A Handbook for Study*, Faith and Order Paper No. 124, WCC Publications, Geneva, 1985; *One God, One Lord, One Spirit: An Explication of the Apostolic Faith Today*, Faith and Order Paper No. 139, WCC Publications, Geneva, 1988; and *Confessing One Faith: An Ecumenical Explication of the Apostolic Faith as it is Confessed in the Nicene-Constantinopolitan Creed (381)*, Faith and Order Paper, No. 153, WCC Publications, Geneva, 1991.

Similarly, *The Catechism of the Catholic Church*, Australian edition, St Pauls, Homebush, 1994, contains much useful material. Part I (276 pages!) of this compendium of Catholic doctrine deals with the articles of the creed.

For further research into the sources of the creeds, an excellent starting point would be Frances Young, *The Making of the Creeds*, SCM, London, 1991. A masterpiece of patristic theology, especially in its treatment of the Greek Fathers, is Thomas F. Torrance, *The Trinitarian Faith*, T. & T. Clark, Edinburgh, 1988. Suitable for the more advanced student, this book establishes the deeply trinitarian structure of Christian faith. Other excellent standard references are J. Stevenson, *Creeds, Councils and Controversies*, Revised edition, SPCK, London, 1989; and J. N. D. Kelly, *Early Christian Creeds*, 3rd edition, Longman, London, 1972.

For a theological overview of creeds, there are a number of fairly accessible popular and complementary presentations. Here I would mention especially two recent books by Protestant scholars: C. E. B. Cranfield, *The Apostles' Creed: A Faith to Live By*, T. & T. Clark, Edinburgh, 1994; and Marianne H. Micks, *Loving the Questions: An Exploration of the Nicene Creed*, Trinity Press International, Valley Forge, 1993. Then, from an Italian Catholic theologian who is consultor on the Vatican Secretariat for Christian Unity, we have Bruno Forte, *A Short Introduction to the Apostles' Creed*, D. M. Groves (trans.), St Pauls, Middlegreen, 1994. One of the last writings of the great European writer, Hans Urs von Balthasar, *Credo: Meditations on the Apostles' Creed*, T. & T. Clark, Edinburgh, 1990, is remarkable for its brevity and depth: many of Balthasar's key theological themes are condensed in this precious little book.

If the reader wishes to move to a deeper level of theological reading, Josef Ratzinger, *Introduction to Christianity*, J. R. Forster (trans.), Burns & Oates, London, 1969, is a modern classic. Equally outstanding is Jan Milic Lochman, *The Faith We Confess: An Ecumenical Dogmatics*, Fortress Press, Philadelphia, 1984. Here this influential Eastern European Evangelical theologian exhibits a faith and a theology purified by the Marxist experience and unfolds the creed in an especially contemporary way.

For the religious educator and theological teacher, the work of the North American Berard Marthaler, *The Creed: Apostolic Faith in Contemporary Theology*, Twenty-Third Publications, Mystic, 1993, is consistently valuable in establishing the historical and the theological context in which the creed can be more fully understood. Nicholas Ayo, C.S.C, in his *Creed as Symbol*, University of Notre Dame Press, Notre Dame, 1989, presents his reflections in an imaginative and deeply reflective manner. The appendix containing various versions and translations of the creed is of special interest. More imaginative still, but soundly theological, is Christopher Morse, *Not Every Spirit: A Dogmatics of Christian Disbelief*, Trinity Press International, Valley Forge, 1994. Morse presents the integrity of Christian belief as the outcome of a process of excluding the variety of errors and misunderstandings that work against the appreciation of Christian faith in all its uniqueness. Wolfhart Pannenberg, *The Apostles' Creed in the Light of Today's Questions*, M. Kohl (trans.), SCM, London, 1972, remains, predictably, a clear and strenuously critical analysis.

For readers who wish to look at still larger contexts in which to explore the creeds—ecological, cosmological, and social—may I recommend my own *An Expanding Theology: Faith in a World of Connections*, E. J. Dwyer, Sydney, 1993. With specific reference to current scientific contexts, I highly recommend John Polkinghorne, *Science and Christian Belief: Theological Reflections of a Bottom-up Thinker. The Gifford Lectures, 1993–4*, SPCK, London, 1994. With his usual vigor and provocativeness, Hans Küng in his *Credo: The Apostles' Creed Explained for Today*, SCM, London, 1993, reflects on the Apostles' Creed, showing a special concern for inter-faith dialogue. A special bonus here consists in Küng's frequent references, along with numerous illustrations, to religious art. The English theologian, Nicholas Lash, in his *Believing Three Ways in One God: A Reading of the Apostles' Creed*, SCM, London, 1992, gives us a novel, though not easily classifiable, work. Lash applies a strongly trinitarian twist to the creed, and he does this in such a way as to accent it as a statement of practical hope.